Instant Pot®
BABY FOOD & TODDLER FOOD
Cookbook

Wholesome Food That Cooks Up Fast in Your Instant Pot® or Other Electric Pressure Cooker

BARBARA SCHIEVING & JENNIFER SCHIEVING MCDANIEL

HARVARD COMMON PRESS

Brimming with creative inspiration, how-to projects, and useful information to enrich your everyday life, Quarto Knows is a favorite destination for those pursuing their interests and passions. Visit our site and dig deeper with our books into your area of interest: Quarto Creates, Quarto Cooks, Quarto Homes, Quarto Lives, Quarto Drives, Quarto Explores, Quarto Gifts, or Quarto Kids.

© 2019 Quarto Publishing Group USA Inc.
Text © 2019 Barbara Schieving and Jennifer Schieving McDaniel
Photography © 2019 Barbara Schieving

First Published in 2019 by The Harvard Common Press, an imprint of The Quarto Group,
100 Cummings Center, Suite 265-D, Beverly, MA 01915, USA.
T (978) 282-9590 F (978) 283-2742 QuartoKnows.com

The Harvard Common Press titles are also available at discount for retail, wholesale, promotional, and bulk purchase. For details, contact the Special Sales Manager by email at specialsales@quarto.com or by mail at The Quarto Group, Attn: Special Sales Manager, 100 Cummings Center, Suite 265-D, Beverly, MA 01915, USA.

23 22 21 20 19   1 2 3 4 5

ISBN: 978-1-55832-969-0

Digital edition published in 2019
eISBN: 978-1-55832-970-6

Library of Congress Cataloging-in-Publication Data

Names: Schieving, Barbara, author. | McDaniel, Jennifer, author.
Title: The instant pot baby food and toddler food cookbook : wholesome food
    that cooks up fast-in any brand of electric pressure cooker / Barbara
    Schieving, Jennifer Schieving McDaniel.
Description: Beverly, MA : Harvard Common Press, 2019. | Includes index.
Identifiers: LCCN 2019006969| ISBN 9781558329690 (trade pbk.) | ISBN
    9781558329706 (ebook)
Subjects: LCSH: Baby foods--Nutrition. | Pressure cooking. | Baby foods. |
    LCGFT: Cookbooks.
Classification: LCC RJ216 .S394 2019 | DDC 641.5/6222--dc23
LC record available at https://lccn.loc.gov/2019006969

Design and Layout: Laura McFadden Design, Inc.

Photography: Barbara Schieving

Printed in China

The information in this book is for educational purposes only. It is not intended to replace the advice of a physician or medical practitioner. Please see your health care provider before beginning any new health program.

Dedication

To all the time-crunched moms and dads doing their best
to feed their families nutritious and delicious food, and to
our families, friends, and readers who share our passion for
pressure cooking and our love of babies and good food—this
cookbook is dedicated to you. Thanks for your support.

Contents

Authors' Note

The first years of a child's life are magical and wondrous. They can also be exhausting and frustrating, as you navigate uncharted territory and strive to do the right things to give your child a great start in life.

When feeding babies or toddlers, it's especially important to ensure they're eating foods that give them the nutrition they need. However, young children require a lot of time and energy, so it's not always easy to schedule time to cook from scratch.

In this cookbook, we've done our best to help make feeding your baby or toddler easier and faster. The electric pressure cooker is a fantastic tool you can use to create healthy, nutritious meals for your family. It also frees up your time; since you're not tied to the stove, you can play with your child or clean up the toys while dinner cooks.

The food habits you want for your children in elementary school and beyond won't magically develop when they hit a certain age—these habits are built from the very beginning. Give your baby or toddler a strong start by using these recipes to introduce them to a wide variety of healthy and delicious fruits, vegetables,

grains, and meats. These are recipes your child will be excited to eat, colorful foods with many different flavors and textures that are served in ways that make mealtime fun.

In addition to the delicious recipes, we've included lots of tips and information gathered from a variety of reliable sources that will help you feel confident that you are doing an awesome job as a parent.

Thanks for being a part of our pressure cooking journey. We hope your children enjoy these foods and you enjoy your meals together as a family.

— BARBARA SCHIEVING
— JENNIFER SCHIEVING MCDANIEL

Introduction

Baby Feeding Basics

Whenever possible, we try to cook our family's meals from scratch; not only is the food better tasting, but we know exactly what ingredients we're eating. If you've ever tried commercial baby food, you'll know that this same principle applies to from-scratch baby food—it just tastes better!

While it can seem intimidating to cook baby food from scratch, an electric pressure cooker makes it easy to cook nutritious food fast. We're here to show you that, with very little planning, you can make your baby food with fresh ingredients without having to spend hours in the kitchen.

Believe it or not, research from the American Academy of Pediatrics indicates that your baby's food preferences start to solidify at just nine months old. Therefore, we believe one of the best things you can do when introducing solid foods is expose your baby to a wide variety of healthy and great-tasting fruits, vegetables, grains, and meats.

Our Approach

As with so many other things relating to babies, many people have strong opinions when it comes to food. Nursing vs. formula feeding, organic vs. conventionally grown, baby-led weaning vs. traditional solids—it can feel exhausting, especially to new parents who want to "get it right" for their baby.

Ultimately, we believe that there are many wonderful approaches to pressure cooking and many great approaches to feeding your baby.

The "right" form of cooking is the one that works with the time you have and the way you want to feed your family—there is no parent-shaming in this book!

We've included a wide variety of recipes in the first half of this book that will take you through baby's first foods to baby's first birthday celebration. These recipes are shaped by our experiences feeding our babies as well as basics recommended by the American Academy of Pediatrics.

We've divided the recipes into sections based on food type to make it easier for you to use. The book starts with recipes for single-ingredient fruits and vegetables, then moves on to grains and legumes, fruit and vegetable blends, and meats and dinners, but how you want to use the recipes is up to you!

Whether you plan to pressure cook just a few foods, batch cook a week's worth of meals, or make every bit of your baby's food from scratch, we will guide you through the process.

Food Introduction Timeline

If you're wondering how to go about introducing solid foods—which food to start with, how much food to give, and how quickly to introduce new foods—you're in good company! Starting solids can feel like a big deal, but it's actually pretty simple. Throughout the process, if you're watching your baby's cues and feeding accordingly, you can feel confident your baby is getting the nutrition they need.

For your convenience, we've compiled a general timeline here based on our pediatricians' recommendations as well as current guidelines given by the American Academy of Pediatrics. Remember that babies' needs can vary widely, so talk with your pediatrician throughout this first year for recommendations tailored specifically to your baby and your family's preferences.

Before solids. The American Academy of Pediatrics generally recommends exclusively feeding babies breast milk or formula for the first six months of life, though there are instances where your pediatrician will recommend starting solids around the four-month mark.

Regardless of age, babies need to achieve certain physical milestones before they can start solids. General signs babies are ready for first foods include:

- They can hold their head steady and turn their head side-to-side as desired.
- They are generally able to sit on their own, with a little support.
- They seem interested in eating or in watching other people eat.
- They open their mouth for food.

☺ Baby's First Feeding

For baby's first feeding, you'll want to choose a time when your baby is happy and a little bit hungry—too hungry and they'll be fussing, too full and they may not be interested in eating.

Prepare your baby's first food. While single grains like rice cereal have traditionally been the first-food of choice, it's up to you to decide whether you'd prefer to start with cereals, fruits, or vegetables. We chose to start with rice cereal thinned with expressed breast milk or formula in hopes that a familiar flavor would lead to a good first food experience. However, others swear by starting with yellow and orange vegetables, then moving into green vegetables, then fruits, and then grains.

Regardless of what you choose to start with, the key is to start with about 1 tablespoon (15 ml) of a single ingredient in a smooth, thin puree. Choose a soft baby spoon and a bib—first feedings can get messy!

When the food is ready, securely strap your baby into a high chair or have your partner hold your baby upright on their lap. Scoop a small spoonful of food and place it in front of your baby. Talk to your baby and model opening your mouth.

If your baby doesn't open their mouth when you present the food, dab a little on their lips; they'll likely lick their lips and get a taste. If they're still not interested, dab a little food on their tray and let them interact with the food on their own terms—chances are their messy, food-coated hands will go right to their mouth.

If the food comes right back out but your baby seems interested in food, keep offering bites of food as long as they're interested. However, if your baby appears agitated when the food comes out, don't force the food on them. You want to keep mealtimes positive. Try again in a day or two and at a different time of day.

The meal is over as soon as your baby starts acting like they're done—common cues include turning away from the spoon, closing their mouth, or pushing food away. Once you notice these signs, put down the baby spoon and congratulate your baby (and yourself) on a successful first feeding!

- They have lost the tongue-thrust reflex and no longer automatically push things back out of their mouth.

When your baby is showing these signs, they're ready to start!

First solids to eight months. Remember, at this earliest stage of eating, solid foods are just a bonus—your baby should still be getting most of their nutrition from breast milk or formula. Offer small amounts of new food—as little as 1 teaspoon (5 ml) at first and work up to 1 tablespoon (15 ml) twice a day around six months, and then up to 8 ounces (225 g) of solids per day by eight months.

Introduce one food at a time and watch for reactions for a few days before introducing another new food. (Mild reactions like gas, diarrhea, or a rash may indicate a food sensitivity. More severe reactions like swelling or vomiting can indicate a food allergy.) Once your baby has eaten one new food for three to five days with no reaction, you can safely leave it in the rotation when you begin introducing another new food. (For example, if you introduce rice cereal and then move on to peaches, you can still serve rice cereal during the waiting period for peaches.)

By the end of this period, your baby should be exposed to a variety of smooth fruits, vegetables, grains, and meats, first served separately and then in combinations.

Eight to ten months. At this stage, breast milk or formula will still be your baby's main source of nutrition, but they will start to take in less milk as they increase their solid-food intake and may drop a bottle or breastfeeding session or two during this period. In these months, babies should progress toward having three meals a day with the rest of the family as well as one or two healthy snacks.

At eight months, your baby should be eating fruits, vegetables, grains, and proteins, and you can begin introducing dairy products like plain yogurt and cottage cheese. (We love mixing dairy with fruit purees and diced fruits!) You can also start giving your baby more textured foods like meats mixed with steamed vegetable bits or grains.

Also, once your baby starts trying to grasp things with their finger and thumb, they're ready to start finger foods! Ideal finger foods are soft and easy to swallow and include bite-size cereals like Cheerios, soft fruits like bananas and avocados, toast, scrambled eggs, steamed vegetables, and cooked pasta. As always, make sure pieces are small and safe.

Ten to twelve months. Continue expanding your baby's diet by adding new flavors and textures. At this point, you can start adding spices to foods—think cinnamon with applesauce or thyme to chicken noodle soup. (Of course, you'll need to start slowly with the seasonings and you'll still need to avoid adding extra sugar or salt.) Continue serving thicker foods, which stick more easily to spoons, as well as finely chopped table foods and finger foods.

Around ten months, you'll need to be teaching your baby to feed themselves with a spoon and to drink from a cup. It's guaranteed to be messy at first, but it's a step they need to take on their way to self-feeding. (And let's be honest—the mess now is worth not having to spoon-feed your kid until they're four!)

Twelve to eighteen months. By twelve months, a significant portion of your baby's diet should come from solid foods. Keep providing healthy foods from the major food groups prepared different ways and in different combinations. Continue giving your baby mashed food or small bites. At twelve months, you also have the green light to introduce honey, raw berries, citrus fruits, and thin layers of creamy nut butter.

At this stage, make sure your baby's meals include plenty of healthy fats; try avocados, eggs, chia seeds, cheese, fish, low-sugar full-fat yogurt, and, of course, full-fat milk.

Unless counseled otherwise by your pediatrician, around twelve months you can start the switch from formula or breast milk to full-fat cow's milk and from bottles to cups. Many babies do best with a gradual change in milk. With some babies, you might replace an ounce (28 ml) of formula with an ounce (28 ml) of cow's milk for a few days, then increase to 2 ounces (60 ml) of cow's milk. Some babies also prefer their milk warmed, so you can slowly decrease the temperature as you dilute it with cow's milk.

Eighteen to twenty-four months. By twenty-four months, your toddler should be eating the same food as the rest of the family, including healthy fruits, vegetables, proteins, and grains—all in small, toddler-size portions.

You'll notice a big improvement in your child's ability to feed themselves during this period; be sure to provide them with many opportunities. In this stage, most toddlers prefer to feed themselves, so plan meals that can be easily diced into small, toddler-friendly finger foods. Your toddler should also have the ability to drink from a cup and to use a spoon, though they may still be messy until age three or four.

Baby Food Safety

There's so much more to food safety than simply dicing food into small pieces and introducing just one new ingredient at a time. For your convenience, we've highlighted a few food-safety items you should be aware of.

Dish up individual servings. Any food that has touched your baby's spoon should be discarded at the end of the meal, regardless of whether you're using store-bought or home-made baby food. The saliva on the spoon can quickly turn your baby's uneaten food into a bacteria breeding ground. To avoid waste, place only what you think your baby will eat into a baby bowl and feed them from the bowl—you can always add more if they're still hungry.

Follow guidelines for safe food preparation. This includes basics like washing your hands well, keeping raw meats away from other food prep, and sterilizing your countertops and cutting boards. Wash and scrub your fruits and vegetables before chopping.

Once cooked, food must be refrigerated or frozen within 2 hours or discarded, and the sooner you can get leftovers in the fridge, the better. Once food is refrigerated, be sure to use or freeze according to USDA baby food standards, which are stricter than food standards for older kids and adults.

COOKED BABY FOOD		
	Refrigerator	**Freezer**
Pureed fruits and vegetables	1 to 2 days	1 to 2 months
Pureed grains and legumes	2 to 3 days	1 to 2 months
Pureed meats and eggs	1 day	1 to 2 months
Meat/vegetable combinations	1 to 2 days	1 to 2 months

Thaw foods in the refrigerator or in cold water, never on the counter at room temperature. And, of course, use your judgment—when in doubt, throw it out!

Know your nitrates. Nitrates are a naturally occurring compound found in soil and well water. In terms of baby food, higher nitrate levels can be found in root and leafy vegetables like carrots, squash, green beans, broccoli, and especially spinach. The American Academy of Pediatrics determined that babies three months and under are most at risk from nitrates, followed by babies six months and under.

Because nitrates occur in the soil, even organic vegetables and commercially prepared baby foods contain them. If you're concerned about nitrate levels in your baby's food, after pressure cooking vegetables, discard the cooking water and use fresh water to make your purees. (Our recipes generally recommend using the cooking water in the purees to retain the vitamins and nutrients that are released into the water during the pressure cooking process.) You can also switch up your food schedule to introduce fruits and grains first and then introduce vegetables when your baby is a little older.

Avoid or limit intake of certain foods. There are a number of foods that are not suitable for babies before age one. These foods are discouraged for a variety of reasons, from contaminants to bacteria to proteins that your baby's digestive system isn't mature enough to handle.

- *Honey.* Pediatricians strongly recommend not giving your baby honey or any food containing honey until after your baby's first birthday. (This includes raw honey, wild honey, commercially prepared honey, and even baked goods containing honey.) Honey is a potential source of the bacteria spores that cause botulism, a dangerous gastrointestinal condition that affects the nervous system. Generally, by age one your baby's intestines will have matured enough that infant botulism is no longer a worry.
- *Rice.* White and brown rice and its derivatives (such as rice milk, rice flour, and brown rice syrup) are a potential source of arsenic for both babies and adults, because rice tends to absorb higher amounts of arsenic from the soil and water. However, rather than avoiding rice altogether, the American Academy of Pediatrics recommends simply being aware and reducing potential arsenic exposure by serving your baby (and family) a wide variety of grains. The FDA also recommends that parents consider options other than rice cereal for first foods.
- *Juice.* In addition to being discouraged due to low fiber and high sugar content, surprisingly, fruit juices are discouraged because they're another potential source of arsenic. Avoid giving juice to babies under twelve months unless recommended by pediatrician—for instance, prune juice to relieve constipation. After twelve months,the recommended amount is just 4 ounces (120 ml) per day served in an open cup.
- *Certain fish.* This one is tricky—some fish can be great for babies, with amino acids and omega-3s; however, many fish have high mercury levels and are not suitable for babies or toddlers. Avoid mackerel, roughy, bluefin tuna, and many shellfish, and check local advisories before feeding your baby freshly caught fish. Recommended fish include codfish, haddock, salmon, tilapia, and canned light tuna.
- *Cow's milk or soy milk.* Although dairy items like yogurt and cheese are encouraged before age one, cow's milk and soy milk should be avoided until after your baby's first birthday. The fats, proteins, and minerals in cow's milk are difficult for babies to digest before their first year, and soy milk does not have the nutrients babies need. (Note that soy milk is different from soy-based infant formulas.) Since too much cow's milk inhibits iron absorption, after twelve months the American Academy of Pediatrics recommends about 16 ounces (475 ml) of full-fat milk a day with a maximum of 24 ounces (700 ml). Soy milk contains lower amounts of calcium, fat, and protein; talk with your pediatrician before introducing it as a replacement for cow's milk.

Test the temperature before serving. While we recommend serving your baby food at a variety of temperatures, be sure to get in the habit of checking the temperature for any food you warm (see the Making Baby Food section for more in-depth guidelines). Microwaves heat food unevenly and create hot spots in the food, and baby food heated on the stovetop may be warmer on the bottom than on top. To address this, stir the food well after warming, let it stand for 30 seconds to a minute, then test the temperature of the food on your lower lip or wrist.

If you're concerned, you can use an instant-read thermometer to make sure the food is below 99°F (37°C) before serving.

Be alert to choking hazards. According to the American Academy of Pediatrics, over 50% of choking episodes occur with food. Here are a few hazards to watch out for:

- *Whole foods.*Whole foods can be potential choking hazards. Foods larger than ½ inch (1.3 cm)—whole blueberries, grapes, cherry tomatoes, nuts, hot dogs, and blocks of cheese—should be sliced into quarters vertically.

- *Stringy foods.* Foods that may be stringy, like beef, orange segments, and celery, should be sliced into very narrow sections and fully separated before serving.
- *Small diced foods.* Other foods can present a choking hazard even when diced small, including diced fruits and vegetables like raw apples and carrots, raisins and other dried fruit, and nuts and seeds.
- *Squishy foods.* Squishy foods like marshmallows, large pieces of bread and rolls, and fruit snacks can also present a choking hazard to babies and toddlers. If you wish to serve these foods, give your child one piece at a time and wait until they swallow before giving them another piece.
- *Nut butters.* Nut butters, including peanut butter, should be thinned with a liquid if served as a dip or spread very thinly on bread.
- *Popcorn, hard candy, and chewing gum.* The American Academy of Pediatrics recommends children avoid popcorn, hard candy, and chewing gum until age four.

Finally, get in the habit of sitting down for meals and giving your full attention to your baby during mealtimes. Don't leave your baby unattended while eating, turn off the TV, and avoid scrolling on your phone during meals. Talk with older children about not giving small foods or toys to your baby.

Watch for reactions to certain foods. Food sensitivities affect the digestive system and are different from actual allergies, which involve the immune system. Still, if your baby has a food sensitivity, it can be hard on their little tummies. Here are some foods to watch out for; if you suspect your baby is sensitive to these foods, give them a rest for a month or two and then try them again.

- *Gas-producing foods.* Beans, lentils, and other high-fiber foods like broccoli and cauliflower are a good source of iron and a natural way to fend off constipation. Unfortunately, their high fiber content may also make your baby gassy. Starches, like breads, grains, and potatoes, as well as some fruits and dairy may also have this effect on your baby's sensitive tummy. Start by giving your baby a small amount

☺ A Note about Allergies

For many years, pediatricians recommended delaying introduction of potential allergens like peanuts, eggs, and dairy until after age one—and even later in children who have a parent or sibling with an allergy. These recommendations began to change in 2008, when the American Academy of Pediatrics announced that there is no convincing evidence that delaying introduction of solid foods, including common allergens, past four to six months will have "a significant protective effect." Recent research may even indicate that early introduction of these allergens actually *lessens* your baby's risk of developing food allergies later in childhood.

However, because the science isn't settled yet, we recommend following your pediatrician's advice regarding food introduction. If your child displays any serious signs of food allergies, such as hives, face and tongue swelling, or vomiting, stop the new food immediately and contact your pediatrician. For severe allergic reactions, call 911.

Substitute any ingredients in this cookbook that your pediatrician has recommended avoiding due to your child's previous reactions to foods or your family history of allergens.

of these foods and then watch them closely for tummy troubles.

- *Acidic fruits and vegetables.* Foods with a high acid content—think strawberries, oranges, pineapples, and tomatoes—may be hard on some babies or cause a mild skin rash around their lips or in their diapers. Generally, these reactions are more common when these fruits and vegetables are served raw than when they've been cooked and pureed.
- *Foods that cause constipation.* Foods particularly likely to cause constipation include starchy foods like breads, rice, and potatoes, as well as bananas, apples, and dairy. In the beginning, just introducing solid foods can sometimes cause problems for babies' sensitive tummies. Prunes, both pureed and juiced, are your first line of defense (if your baby will take them). You can also introduce more high-fiber foods into your child's diet. If constipation is more than an occasional problem, be sure to talk to your pediatrician.
- *Water. Wa*ter should not be a significant part of your baby's diet; your baby should receive all of the fluids they need from breast milk or formula. Exceptions to this rule are when it's really hot outside, if your baby appears constipated, or once your baby is old enough to practice drinking from a cup. Talk to your pediatrician if you have questions.

Baby Mealtime Tips

Keep in mind that we're not doctors or psychologists—we're just a mother-daughter team that has done our best to get healthy foods in our babies without stressing too much! However, after all these years feeding kids, we do have a few tricks up our sleeves, supported by recent guidelines from pediatricians and parenting experts. (See the Resources section for some of our favorites.)

Make mealtimes upbeat, affectionate, and relaxed. Let's face it, mealtimes with babies can feel long and frustrating—especially when your baby makes a huge mess or just flat-out rejects the foods you're trying to serve.

However, since the main goal of introducing solid foods is to set the foundation for a healthy lifetime relationship with food, do what you can to establish an upbeat, relaxed approach to mealtimes for both you and your baby.

For parents, remember that a big part of keeping mealtimes relaxed is planning meals ahead of time and based around your schedule. Plan to tackle important skills like self-feeding when you're not in a rush and have time to give your baby a full-on bath if needed. If the mess stresses you out, put a splat mat under the high chair or strip your baby down to their diaper. When eating out or with friends and extended family, pull out less-messy finger foods and only give your baby a little at a time to reduce messes.

For your baby, so much of their experience depends on their personality: some babies are eager to taste anything you put in front of them, while others clamp their mouths shut at the sight of a spoon. Some babies eat quickly, others take their time; some love purees, others prefer finger foods; some eat quite a bit, others just nibble. No matter what your baby's approach is to eating, help them stay relaxed by following their cues. Don't force your baby to finish food they don't like or eat if they're not hungry. End the meal once their attention has waned.

Foster connection at mealtimes. Family meals are an important time for connection, especially as your children grow. Starting with their very first meals, make mealtimes a connection point with your baby.

Turn off the TV, put away your cell phone, and minimize other distractions. Make eye contact and talk to your baby throughout the feeding process. Once your baby begins to vocalize, "chat" back and forth with them about the foods they're eating. Acknowledge when they like or don't like something.

Another way to foster connection is to establish a routine around eating and give your baby clear signals throughout. Whether you use sign language or sing songs, use clear signals to indicate the start and end of mealtimes as well as different points in the meal, like getting in the high chair or putting on the bib. We used simple signs (like *more, all done, milk*), and there's just something adorable about watching your baby enthusiastically sign "more" before each bite. We found that signs helped make our babies active participants in the feeding process and began opening communication even before they could speak.

Offer the same food multiple times. Research from the American Academy of Pediatrics has shown that it can take as many as twenty exposures to a new food before a baby accepts it. If your baby doesn't like a food, don't force them to eat it. However, don't take it off the menu either! Wait a week or two and then try it again. And again and again, as necessary.

Also, try serving the food in different ways— mix it with cereal, yogurt, or cottage cheese; blend it with another food that your baby prefers; or try dicing it small and serving it as a finger food. Keep trying!

Serve meals strategically. Offer new or less-favorite foods first and save favorite foods for later in the meal. Similarly, serve vegetables and lower-sugar foods first then switch to sweeter foods like fruits.

Also, apply this principle throughout the day: serve new or less-favorite foods when your baby is awake and in a good mood, and save favorite, familiar foods for when your baby is tired or more likely to be fussy.

Set up healthy habits. The American Academy of Pediatrics recommends parents serve fruits or veggies at every meal. Exposing your baby to many different fresh flavors and textures and to foods made from fresh produce and home-cooked meats teaches them to eat right and love real foods from the beginning. This is a healthy habit that will serve them well throughout their life. (And it might even encourage you to add more fruits and vegetables to your meals as well.)

Making Baby Food

Here are the basics you need to know to get started making nutritious, delicious foods for your baby.

Cooking Baby Food

The recipes walk you through the process of making the purees. Prepare your ingredients by washing your produce well, rinsing your grains and beans, and trimming your meats. Cook the food according to the recipe. Don't be afraid to experiment with the recipes—if you find adding a minute or two at high pressure helps your foods blend better, go for it! Or if you want your purees to be a little more textured for older eaters, take a minute or two off the cook time. (It's baby food, not fine French cooking. Just make sure that meats are cooked to the safe internal temperatures on page 25.)

Once the foods are cooked, we like to transfer them to a bowl to cool and reserve the cooking water in a glass or a measuring cup with a pour spout. This frees you up to either start another batch of food in the pressure cooker or clean your pressure cooker while the food cools.

When you're ready to puree, make sure you don't overfill your blender or food processor. Add enough liquid that the foods can blend without being too thin. If you want your purees to be smooth like commercial baby food, you'll need to use a high-powered blender. Blend at a low speed for about 10 seconds to break down the ingredients, then blend for another 20 seconds at a high speed for smooth purees.

The baby food recipes in this book were pureed using a high-powered blender to determine the minimum amount of water needed for each recipe. If you are using a traditional blender, you'll likely need to add more water to your baby foods to blend them to a smooth consistency.

If you don't have a high-powered blender but still want your purees as smooth as possible, just puree the foods as smooth as you can, then pass them through a fine-mesh strainer.

If you're serving the baby food immediately, make sure it's cooled enough to be safe for your baby. Refrigerate the portion you plan to serve in the next day or two, then transfer the remainder of the baby food to freezer-safe containers.

Making multiple foods in one session. When using the steamer basket for purees, start with the easiest recipe to prepare. While the first batch is in the pressure cooker, start preparing the ingredients for the next batch. When your first batch is finished cooking, empty the contents of the steamer basket, rinse out the pot and steamer basket, and start the next batch. (If you're using the steamer basket again, don't forget to add the cup (235 ml) of water in the bottom before locking the lid! It can be easy to forget when you're making many foods in one session.) If you're making any meats, be sure to save those for the end of the pressure cooking session.

Make multiple purees at the same time. You can use pot-in-pot cooking to make more than one puree at once. For instance, using wide-mouth mason jars, you can make four smaller batches of different purees at the same time. To do this, you need to choose recipes that have similar cook times, such as apples and pears. See 4-in-1 Single-Ingredient Purees (page 49) for an example of this process.

Freezing, Storing, and Thawing Baby Food
Make sure you have selected a container that is freezer-safe, particularly if you're using glass containers to freeze your baby foods. Before freezing, tightly wrap trays with plastic wrap or secure the lid tightly in place on your freezer-safe containers.

If you've made several batches of baby food, use masking tape and a permanent marker to label the freezer container. (You may think you'll know which puree is in which container, but many purees can look similar and it can get hard to remember a week later. Make things easy on yourself!)

Once the food is frozen solid, you can transfer the portions to a ziplock bag. Again, make sure the bag is labeled with the type of food and the date it was cooked. Remove as much air as possible from the bag before sealing tightly. Store baby food away from the fridge or freezer doors to make sure the food stays as cold as possible. Be sure to use or discard the baby food according to the recommended schedule on page 10.

Sometimes baby food purees can develop ice crystals on top; this is fine and won't affect the quality of the foods. If you suspect some purees have developed freezer burn, the USDA says that these foods are still safe to eat, just cut away freezer-burned portions for texture reasons.

Thawing baby food puree. We recommend getting in the habit of planning your baby's meals the night before since the easiest way to thaw your purees is to place them in the fridge overnight. Simply remove the frozen purees you plan to serve, place them in individual bowls, cover, and they'll be ready to serve in the morning. (Do not refreeze foods once they have thawed.) Sometimes purees defrosted in the refrigerator will have liquids separate out. Give these purees a good stir to reincorporate the liquids.

Some babies are happy to eat foods right out of the refrigerator; however, others prefer their purees to be warmed, at least at first. There are several ways to warm the food—use whichever method aligns with your parenting style.

- *Warm water.* Fill a shallow bowl with hot water. Place the small bowl of baby food puree inside the shallow bowl, checking to make sure the hot water does not come over the top of the baby food bowl. Allow the baby food to sit until it reaches your desired temperature. (This method also works if you forgot to remove the baby food from the freezer the night before; it just takes a little longer to warm through, so you may need to replace the water.)
- *Stovetop.* Place the baby food in a small saucepan. Turn the heat on low and stir the baby food frequently. Add a little liquid if the baby food thickens before it's

heated to your desired temperature. Be sure to stir well and test the temperature before serving to your baby.

- *Microwave.* Place the baby food in a glass dish and cook at 50 percent power for 15 seconds. Stir well to avoid hot spots and test the temperature before serving to your baby.

Also, be aware that freezing may change the structure of foods; in some instances, purees that were perfect fresh may take on a different texture when thawed. Some babies won't mind the changes in texture; others may be more sensitive. Here's what you can expect:

- *Fruits and vegetables.*Some fruits and vegetables defrost a little watery, others defrost a little thick. Before deciding to add water, be sure to mix the thawed puree well. For older eaters, you can mix in some diced or mashed fruits to help thicken the puree and change up the texture.
- *Grains and legumes.* We recommend freezing cooked grains and legumes whole in individual, flattened portions. Once frozen solid, transfer frozen portions to a single freezer bag. After defrosting, use a food mill and puree until smooth. (Despite our best efforts, no matter what methods we tried, frozen pureed cereals turned rubbery, watery, and unappealing when defrosted.) Freezing grains and legumes whole also allows you to stir them into purees to add texture for older eaters.
- *Meats and dinners.* Freezing pureed meats may change the texture and consistency of the puree. Much like the fruits and vegetables, mix the thawed purees well before deciding to add more water. If you wish, you can also freeze the cooked meats in individual portions before pureeing.

Mix and match. When thawing baby foods, you don't have to keep everything separate. Thaw a portion of rice with a portion of sweet peas or chicken to make a great meal for your eight-month-old. Combine different flavors of fruit purees with yogurt to make a fun baby breakfast smoothie!

Sterilizing in Your Pressure Cooker

If you wish, you can sterilize or sanitize your bottles and pump parts in your electric pressure cooker. Some models of pressure cookers, like the Instant Pot Duo Plus, have a built-in Sterilize feature, while other brands direct you to use a Steam setting or even the High Pressure setting.

Unfortunately, there is very little official guidance from the major brands on the sterilization process to ensure that your items are sterilized. In addition, there are differences in opinion regarding whether pressure cookers get hot enough or achieve a high enough pressure to truly sanitize (250°F [121°C] at 15 psi), so some people consider this a "sanitizing" feature. Ultimately, not enough testing has been done on sterilizing in the pressure cooker, so we can't officially recommend it at this time.

However, if you are interested in using the pressure cooker for sanitizing baby bottles or binkies, the common practices are as follows:

- Before sterilizing, make sure your baby bottles, jars, pump parts, pacifiers, and utensils are safe for steaming. (Generally, the packaging inserts that come with these items will include information on whether they can be boiled and for how long.)
- Wash these items in warm, soapy water, then rinse well.
- Place 1 cup (235 ml) water in your pressure cooker, then use a trivet or steamer basket to elevate the items above the water when steaming. Don't place directly on the bottom of the pressure cooking pot, and don't overfill.
- If your pressure cooker has a Sterilize function, select Sterilize adjusted to high; if not, select Steam or High Pressure and 2 minutes cook time. Use a quick pressure release. (You can increase the cook time or use a natural pressure release if you wish, but be mindful of the items you're steaming; some items may warp at longer cook times.)

Useful Equipment for Making Baby Food

Although we've listed a number of items that will make cooking baby food easier, they're not all mandatory. Try making baby food with what you already have on hand and see what items you'd like to add to your collection. Don't feel like you have to run out and buy all of these at once—save that money for diapers!

Blender. Not all blenders are created equal. If you want to make your homemade baby food as smooth as store-bought baby food, you'll need a high-powered blender like Blendtec or Vitamix. These blenders have powerful motors that can handle blending thicker foods with less liquid, and their large blender jars also give you the ability to make large batches of baby food at once.

Immersion blender. Immersion blenders, also called "stick blenders," let you blend directly in the pressure cooking pot or wide-mouth mason jar without having to worry about spilling or waste from transferring to a separate blender jar. (If you have a nonstick cooking pot, be careful not to scratch your pot with an immersion blender.) Although these appliances are powerful and convenient, they don't blend food quite as smoothly or as uniformly as a high-powered blender and generally require additional water to blend. However, we love immersion blenders for making thicker, more textured purees for older eaters.

Food processor. Food processors are also an option for making baby food purees. These machines use a sharp blade to chop and puree foods, and they come in many sizes. Some people prefer using a food processor for making purees because some food processors can use less water and make purees a little thicker; others prefer blenders for their uniform consistency. Try what you have before you decide. We like food processors to make quick work of chopping cheeses and meats for older eaters but prefer blenders for making smooth baby food purees.

Food mill. Food mills are a great way to puree and strain at the same time. These gadgets come in a wide variety of sizes, from several quarts on down, and have historically been used for canning. If you plan to make baby foods in big batches and don't mind an arm workout, this will be a wonderful addition to your kitchen. Generally, food mills work well with softer fruits, vegetables, grains, and legumes—many food mills can even filter out the seeds in fruit purees. However, they may struggle to grind meats or stringy vegetables like green beans.

For making a single serving of baby food, skip the larger mills in favor of a baby food mill. These smaller mills come in both electric and hand-crank models and allow you to grind up small amounts of food. We particularly love the baby food mills for grinding grains. The results won't be as smooth as commercial cereals, but we love them for making single-serving meals when baby is ready for some texture.

Masher. Whether you purchase a baby food masher or just use the regular-old potato masher you have around your house, this tool is perfect for older babies who can handle a bit of texture in their soft foods. If you want to get fancy, try a ricer—they're perfect for pressing potatoes and other soft foods into fine purees.

Fine-mesh sieve. Also called a "strainer," this kitchen gadget comes in a number of sizes. For baby food, we prefer a small-size strainer because it is less mess to clean up. Although it can be time-consuming, pushing soft fruit and vegetable purees through the sieve with the back of a spoon allows you to remove seeds, skins, or strings.

Kitchen shears. Although this kitchen gadget isn't necessarily pressure cooker–specific, it is by far our most-used tool for feeding babies finger foods. Whether you call them "shears" or "scissors," these sharp, oversized kitchen scissors make it a snap to snip meats, veggies, and breads into baby-friendly bites either before or after pressure cooking.

Baby food freezer trays. Once you've made the baby food, you'll need something to freeze it in. Although there are a variety of products you can use, from simple ice cube trays to plastic pouches, for younger eaters, we love the baby food freezer trays that allow us to freeze purees in small ¾-ounce (21 g) cubes, which minimizes food waste. For older eaters, we love the round BPA-free silicone baby food trays. Not only are they great for freezing baby food into larger 2-ounce (55 g) servings, but the round trays fit perfectly in a 6-quart (5.7 L) pressure cooker, allowing you to continue to use them after your baby has outgrown purees. (For instance, use them to make many of the breakfasts in the Toddler section.)

Other noteworthy feeding accessories. Although not necessary for making baby food, there are three other items we'd like to mention here:

- First, find a few good spoons for feeding your baby. For first foods, we love the tiny rubber-coated spoons with a shallow bowl. These spoons make it so easy to scoop a small amount of food, and they protect your baby's gums. However, once baby starts reaching for their own spoon, we prefer shorter, wider spoons with slightly deeper bowls. (The first-foods spoons tend to have longer handles that babies can gag themselves with.)
- Second, we couldn't live without a splat mat, which goes under the high chair and makes for easy cleanup after meals.
- Finally, compartmentalized serving dishes are awesome for feeding older babies and toddlers. Whether you use an ice cube tray, divided plates, or silicone baby food containers, consider getting a dish with small compartments that will allow you to put different foods in each compartment. This gives your child some control over what they eat and how they eat it.

☺ Resources

If you're interested in reading in depth about your child's nutrition and development or in learning more about making baby food, we've included some of our favorite books and websites that we've consulted as we've raised our own children. These books represent a range of perspectives on these issues, so some of them may be a better fit for your parenting style than others.

Books

The American Academy of Pediatrics. 2014 *Caring for Your Baby and Young Child, 6th edition.* Edited by Steven P. Shelov and Tanya Remer Altmann.

The American Academy of Pediatrics. 2012 *Nutrition: What Every Parent Needs to Know*, 2nd edition. Edited by William H. Dietz and Loraine Stern.

Nimali Fernando and Melanie Potock. 2015 *Raising a Healthy, Happy Eater: A Parent's Handbook: A Stage-by-Stage Guide to Setting Your Child on the Path to Adventurous Eating.*

Ellyn Satter. 2000. *Child of Mine: Feeding with Love and Good Sense*, revised edition.

William Sears, Martha Sears, Robert Sears, and James Sears. 2013 *The Baby Book: Everything You Need to Know About Your Baby from Birth to Age Two*, revised edition.

Websites

www.healthychildren.org
www.askdrsears.com
www.familydoctor.org
www.foodsafety.gov
www.wholesomebabyfood.com
www.superhealthykids.com

Toddler Feeding Basics

The toddler years are a magical time as your babies learn to express themselves, become more playful, and grow into their unique personalities. However, the same things that make these years wonderful can also make them difficult, as these little people begin to assert strong opinions over what they'll wear, do, and eat.

And the thing about eating is that it can seem like toddlers do it *all. day. long.* The American Academy of Pediatrics recommends toddlers eat three meals a day along with two to three healthy snacks. Some days, it can feel like your toddler is hungry again before you've even cleaned up the previous meal—and that doesn't even account for making healthy meals for yourself!

So, how to cook healthy meals your toddler will eat without losing your mind or spending the entire day in the kitchen? The key is finding quick, easy-to-cook, and healthy meals your toddler will want to eat; in other words, the kind of meals your pressure cooker is naturally suited for.

You'll love the recipes in this section, which are made pressure cooker fast and teach you how to cook main and side dishes at the same time, ultimately getting you out of the kitchen a little quicker.

Our Approach

Your child's food habits start early and are a unique combination of their innate prefer-ences and their personal experiences with food. Just as you teach your toddler to drink from a cup and eat with utensils, you need to teach them to love the healthy foods your family eats.

The recipes in this section are designed to make family mealtime a time that everyone can look forward to.

Cook family meals. We don't believe parents need to cook separate meals for toddlers and adults—it's enough work to get one meal on the table! Yet, it can be particularly disheartening to make a big batch of food, only to have your toddler turn up their nose—or worse, throw it on the floor! Therefore, the recipes in this book are designed to make a single meal for smaller families of three or four, since larger families will likely have grown beyond making meals specifically for their toddlers' tastes.

Customize for your toddler. We've taken our family's favorite recipes and toned down the seasonings and sugar content to introduce your toddler to grown-up food without overwhelming their sensitive palates. (Think of these recipes as training wheels for family eating.) We have also included several points where you can remove a portion specifically for your toddler before finishing the recipe, allowing you to enjoy a grown-up meal and still serve certain foods on the side to help your toddler grow accustomed to the meal.

Make it your way. If you know your toddler hates a certain ingredient, switch it out! Just be sure that when you make a substitution, you're trading for another ingredient that's similar in size, texture, and cooking needs. (For instance, subbing frozen corn for frozen peas would work great, while subbing peas for fresh asparagus or large broccoli florets wouldn't work well.)

The same principles apply for thickeners (use twice as much flour as cornstarch), grains (white rice cooks much faster than brown rice), and meats (ground chicken and ground beef have similar cooking needs, while diced chicken cooks much faster than diced beef or whole chicken breasts). Similarly, if you prefer a sauce or soup thicker or thinner than the one specified, add or reduce the liquids added after pressure cooking.

Spice it up. Many of these recipes give you a range of sugar and spices you can add, allowing you to choose how much of these ingredients you want. These recipes try to strike a good balance between being intentionally mild for your toddlers but not so bland that parents won't enjoy eating with them. If a dish is too mild for your tastes, add a little extra seasoning to your portion. Or, on the other hand, if the spices are still too much for your toddler, walk things back even further.

Keep it simple. Mealtimes not only test toddlers' adaptability to new textures and flavors, but they also test toddlers' fine motor skills. We've tried to keep these recipes easy for toddlers to eat, including extra-thick breakfasts, soups, and sauces that stick to the spoon or bread when dipped. As necessary, customize the consistency to your family's tastes. In addition, many lunches and dinners go into the pressure cooker bite-sized, minimizing the amount of dicing you have to do once the food is cooked.

Toddler Mealtime Tips

Many of the baby food safety recommendations and mealtime tips (pages 10-14) apply to toddlers. As your toddler grows, there are additional games you can play and tricks you can try to keep your toddler interested in eating and open to trying new things. As always, you'll want to defer to your pediatrician for help addressing concerns specific to your toddler.

Keep foods small to avoid choking hazards. As inconvenient as it may be to break out the knife and chop food to bits *every single meal*, it's still the safest way to feed your toddler. Many of the Baby Food Safety rules (page 10) still apply to toddlers. Quarter carrots, hot dogs, grapes, and tomatoes vertically, then cut into small bites. Chop or mash other fruits, vegetables, breads, and meats into ½-inch (1.3 cm) pieces or smaller. Foods that may be stringy should be sliced into very narrow sections and fully separated before serving. Nut butters should be thinned with a liquid if served as a dip or spread very thinly on bread.

Toddlers who tend to stuff their mouths with food should only be given a few bites on their plate at a time. And be aware that this isn't a short-term rule—toddlers can't reliably chew their food until age four.

We've found a good pair of kitchen shears makes life much easier when it comes to quickly dic-ing toddler meals.

Offer the same food multiple times and cooked different ways. Again, remember it can take as many as twenty exposures to a new food before a toddler begins to accept it. Now that your toddler is older, you can also vary the textures and spices of the food in question. Preparing food different ways helps you figure out the flavors, colors, and cooking methods your child prefers. For instance, some kids don't like raw veggies, some don't like steamed veggies, some don't like green veggies, and some don't care how the veggie is prepared as long as they can dip it. Keep serving it until you find a way they like it.

Incorporate the five senses. For toddlers, meals are about much more than taste—before they even put the food in their mouths, it has to pass a visual inspection as well as the sniff test. Don't worry, though! Your toddler doesn't expect photo-worthy meals and can be happy with dividing the meals into separate compartments. (This principle led directly to our approach in the lunch section of the cookbook where each of the major ingredients of a grown-up meal is served à la carte in separated trays.)

Keep an eye on the clock. A hungry toddler is often a cranky, uncooperative toddler. Some of our family's biggest food battles have happened after the kids have gone *a little* too long between meals. (And then they don't eat, even though food is the only thing that will help them feel better, and the fussing goes on much longer than it should.)

Once a meal begins, toddlers have a limited attention span for eating. After their initial hunger is satisfied, giving them too long at the table often results in them finding messy ways to entertain themselves. (Even now, one of Jennifer's kids will sit at the table picking at food for *hours* if given the chance.) Creating a general, flexible schedule with set beginning and end times for meals and snacks will make things easier on all of you in the long run.

Watch out for big swings in eating habits. It's strange—sometimes your toddler can literally out-eat you; other times, it seems like your toddler exists on nothing but air and crackers. These swings can be unsettling, but they're normal toddler behavior. Generally, their eating will even out over the course of a few days or weeks. Talk to your pediatrician if you're worried about weight or nutrition, but if your pediatrician is happy, your toddler is good to go. To reduce waste, we generally serve very small portions to toddlers and let them ask for seconds (and thirds) if they're hungry.

Also, don't expect toddlers to be consistent with their food preferences! Toddlers can be irrationally obsessed with a food one week and reject it the next. It's frustrating ("But just five minutes ago you *asked* me to cook you this!?"), but it's normal life with toddlers.

For younger toddlers, we've had good luck with pairing new foods with favorite foods, serving multiple healthy side dishes at mealtimes, and letting them feed themselves regardless of the mess. For older toddlers, offering choices of foods before cooking helps feed their need for independence and makes them more willing to eat what you've cooked.

Make mealtimes playful family time. When possible, sit down for meals with your toddler. Sharing meals is a great time for connection and fun, and it gives you the chance to model healthy eating habits. (It also allows you to keep an eye on the mess and intervene before it gets out of hand.)

We've also found that kids eat best when there's an element of fun involved. Those same "airplane noise" games that worked for your babies can be adjusted to work for your toddler. Games we've had good luck with include:

- Have your toddler "steal" their food from you. For this one, you bring your chair up close to the toddler's chair and scoop a bite up off their plate. Say something like, "Look, I'm going to eat this delicious bite of broccoli!" and then pretend you're raising the food to your mouth while actually putting it in front of your toddler. If your toddler is into the game, they'll lean in and take "your" bite off the spoon. Once they've done this, pretend to look around for the "missing" food, then scoop another bite and repeat.

- Pretend your toddler is an animal and the food is their animal food. ("Look, baby shark, some delicious fish. Can you catch it?") This game is easily modified to match their current obsession like construction trucks eating gas or princesses eating at the royal tea party).
- Ask your toddler to take different sizes of bites. ("Show me a grandma bite, a baby bite, a big daddy bite, a dinosaur bite," and so on.)
- Reverse roles by having your toddler try to feed you a bite of something and you pretend not to like it. Make it clear you're being silly, bring in elements of their behavior when they refuse to try something, and encourage them to be the parent trying to get you to eat. Let the toddler "convince" you to put the food in your mouth and make a big deal of stopping your fuss and changing your mind to liking the food. (This game works best for older toddlers.)

Keep in mind that some toddlers will respond better to some games than others and that the games that work well for one kid may not work for another. However, introducing play into mealtime can significantly help your toddler stay interested in the meal and help them be more willing to try new foods. Find what works for you!

Prepare for picky phases. Some kids are easygoing eaters; others . . . not so much. You'll also find that each kid swings in their own range, so even easygoing eaters will have picky periods where a once-favorite food is no longer acceptable. Don't be offended—it's not you, it's them.

In our experience, pickiness comes from two places: genuine uncertainty about or dislike of certain flavors/textures and a need to exert control. For the first issue, we've found that it works well to acknowledge a food is unfamiliar or isn't a favorite and involve them in figuring out if there's a way they can make the food work for them.

As far as control is concerned, let's face it: no matter how convenient it would be, you can't *make* your toddler eat. While as a parent you

Go-to Phrases to Help Take the Battles Out of Eating

We've all had moments where absolutely nothing could convince our kids to eat a certain food. However, we've stumbled on the following phrases that have helped us—maybe they can be a starting point for you and your family. (These work best with older toddlers.)

"It's not my taste."

There's nothing like the feeling of being over to dinner at someone's house and having your toddler yell "YUCKY!" at full volume. Around your dinner table, have conversations about how different people like different foods and how certain foods aren't inherently "yucky" or "yummy." Bring up your child's favorite foods and the people they know who don't like those foods. (Toddlers really enjoy it when they like a food that's not Mom or Dad's taste.)

Eventually, they understand that if they don't like a certain food, it just isn't their taste at the moment—and that's OK! For us, this has reduced power struggles around eating and has also led to less fussing when we cook one of their less-favorite meals.

"You don't have to like it, you just have to try it to see if your tastes have changed."

Usually, you have a pretty good idea if your children will like a meal. For the foods you suspect will be met with resistance, try to have a few sides on the table you know they'll like—favorite fruits, vegetables, breads, or crackers. Give your toddler a very small serving of everything on the table and emphasize that you aren't sure whether their tastes have changed, so you'd like them to try just one good bite.

Generally, most kids will take a bite and leave the rest on their plate. If they've done one good bite, let them fill up on the side dishes they enjoy. Occasionally, though, there's an excited, "Mom, my tastes have changed!" When that happens, really celebrate and talk about how much they're growing up.

"How can we make it more your taste?"

Occasionally, you'll be caught off-guard when your toddler declares something is not their taste—especially when the meal has ingredients they like or when it was a meal they used to ask for often. In those instances, when you don't have other options on the table, ask your toddler to think of ideas that would help make the meal more to their liking.

Let your children know that you don't make separate meals for kids and parents in your house. However, also let them know that you are willing to try simple, no-cook ways to modify the meal, like turning salads into sandwiches, serving sauces on the side, picking out certain ingredients (after trying one), cutting foods into different shapes, or adding ingredients to their foods. Usually adding ingredients consists of adding salt, pepper, butter, or ketchup, but occasionally they'll ask for off-the-wall toppings like sour cream on breakfast foods or sprinkles on a baked potato. In those instances, let them try a bite with a small amount of the desired topping on it first and let them add more if they still want to.

Giving your child control of how to modify a meal can cut down on mealtime battles because it puts you on the same team looking for a solution you can both live with.

have a few power plays, like punishing (not a great option because it turns mealtimes into regular power struggles) or bribing (also not great because it makes every mealtime an exhausting negotiation on the number of bites), the most effective long-term solution is finding positive ways to encourage your toddler to eat.

In addition to the games mentioned previously, we've had great luck in "rebranding" foods by riffing on the name of a favorite food. For instance, a toddler may swear they hate pasta with pesto sauce, but they'll *love* eating green mac and cheese (aka pesto with a little moz-zarella on top). So you might consider serving green mac, tomato mac (regular spaghetti sauce), and cheese mac (actual macaroni and cheese) and see what happens.

Let others step in. With toddlers, there will be times where they just won't eat for you, no matter what foods you serve or games you try. It can be particularly maddening to deal with this pushback day after day (after day), and you might be exasperated enough to try bribing or punishing. In these instances, call on your support squad! Ask a trusted friend or relative to feed your child for a meal or two as needed. Sometimes Grandma or a favorite uncle has the magic touch, and your toddler will happily eat things for them that they'd never eat for you. So let them step in while you enjoy a meal in peace! Time away can be just as important for the toddler as it is for the parent.

Pressure Cooker Essentials

The recipes in this cookbook are written to work in all brands of electric pressure cookers, including the Instant Pot. While you may already be familiar with the pressure cooking terminology and settings for your specific device, for your convenience, we've included a brief guide explaining how we've used these terms in this cookbook.

Pressure Cooker Parts

It might look complicated initially, but your electric pressure cooker is actually pretty simple when you get to know it, and all brands have similar components. For questions specific to your particular model, check your user manual.

Housing. This is the outer part of the pressure cooker that contains the buttons and the heating element and is connected to the cord. *DO NOT add ingredients directly to the housing or you may permanently damage your pressure cooker.*

Cooking pot. This is the inner removable pot, and it's where the magic happens. While you're adding the ingredients to the cooking pot, you can treat it like you treat any pot on the stove—for example, lifting it up off the heating element to slow the cooking. Once you lock the lid in place, however, you'll be unable to access this pot until the pressure is released.

Sealing ring. This large flexible ring attaches to the underside of the lid. When the lid is locked, the sealing ring prevents steam from escaping, allowing the machine to build pressure inside the pot.

Float valve and mini gasket. This small valve fits inside the lid and is paired with a miniature silicone gasket. When your machine reaches pressure, steam pushes the float valve up and seals the pressure cooker, locking the lid until the float valve drops again, indicating that the pressure inside the cooker has been released.

Pressure release switch. This piece is located on the lid and controls how the pressure inside the pot can escape. In one position, it will seal the steam inside your electric pressure cooker and in another it will allow the steam to release quickly. (Depending on your model of electric pressure cooker, this may be called a *switch*, *valve*, or *button*, but the function is identical.)

Cook Settings

While each model of pressure cooker has different buttons and different functions, most of them are just preset cook times for different foods. *Remember, your pressure cooker CANNOT actually sense what you are cooking and CANNOT tell you when the food in your pot is cooked through.* Since the recipes in this cookbook were developed for all brands of electric pressure cookers, we avoid the preset buttons and use only the following settings:

High Pressure/Manual/Pressure Cook. This setting tells the machine to cook at high pressure. When a recipe says, "Select High Pressure and 5 minutes cook time," this will be the setting you use. (The exact name of this setting will depend on the model of electric pressure cooker you own. If your model of pressure cooker doesn't have a manual setting, consult your user guide and choose the preset button with the closest time to the time in the recipe.)

Sauté/Simmer/Browning. This setting allows you to use the cooking pot like any other stovetop pot. Use this setting with the lid off. (Depending on your brand of electric pressure cooker, you may have separate buttons for each heat level or a single button that can adjust the heat level up or down as desired. Some brands don't have a Sauté button, and users select a preset button with the lid off.)

Keep Warm. When the cook time ends, many electric pressure cookers will automatically switch to the Keep Warm setting. Be aware that the contents of your pot will continue to cook as long as this setting is on. This setting can be useful; however, we recommend turning this setting off or unplugging the pressure cooker if you're prone to forgetting to remove the cooking pot from the housing once the meal is complete. And, of course, be sure to turn off your pressure cooker when you're done using it.

Pressure Release Methods

After the cook time has ended, the timer will sound. At this point, the recipe will direct you to release the pressure using the following methods:

Quick pressure release. When the cook time ends, turn the pressure release switch to Venting and watch the pressure cooker release a jet of steam. Be sure to position your pressure cooker so that the steam vents away from your cabinets and avoid placing your face or hands directly over the vent, since the steam can burn. If liquid or foam starts coming out of the vent,

return the switch to the Sealed position for a minute or two, then try venting the pressure again. Wait until the pressure is completely released, the float valve drops, and the lid unlocks easily before trying to open the lid.

Natural pressure release. When the cook time ends, just leave the pressure release switch in the Sealed position. The pressure will release slowly, with no visible jet of steam or noise. With this method, the only way you'll know the pressure is fully released is the float valve will drop and the lid will unlock easily. (It's a bit anticlimactic in comparison to the quick release.)

Many recipes combine these release methods, instructing you to allow the pressure to release naturally for a certain amount of time, then finish with a quick pressure release. To do this, simply wait the specified number of minutes, then turn the switch from Sealed to Venting to release any remaining pressure.

Pressure Cooking Accessories

A few simple accessories will make cooking a little easier and will help you get even more time savings from your pressure cooker. Some of these items will come with your pressure cooker, and you may already own other accessories that can be used in your pressure cooker. Generally, as long as it's an oven-safe dish that fits on a trivet inside the inner cooking pot with room for steam to rise around the dish, it's good to go.

The following accessories are ones we've used in this cookbook; however, you don't need all of these all at once. If you're thinking of purchasing some accessories, we recommend starting with an instant-read thermometer, for food safety, and a round cake pan and trivet, since many of our recipes use the pot-in-pot cooking method. Add the other accessories as your budget allows.

Double-stack pot. This accessory is newer to the pressure cooking world; essentially, it's a set of stackable pans where the top pan works as a lid to the bottom pan and fits perfectly inside the pressure cooking pot. This pot gives you a little more freedom for pot-in-pot cooking and is essential for the Sauce-Separate Lasagna (page 159).

Extra silicone ring. Because the silicone ring sometimes takes on the smell of your most recent meal, we prefer to have at least two silicone rings for our pressure cooker: one for making savory, spicy, or strong-smelling foods and another for breakfasts, fruits, and desserts.

Half-size Bundt pan. A half-size (6-cup [1410 ml]) Bundt pan without a large rim fits perfectly in a 6-quart (5.4 L) pressure cooker. This pan allows foods like the Blueberries and Cream Baked French Toast (page 117) to cook more quickly and evenly than they would in a simple cake pan.

Instant-read thermometer. Whether it's a fork-style or pen-style thermometer, this important food-safety tool helps you ensure that foods have reached a safe internal temperature. Because cuts of meat can vary widely in size and thickness, it is always wise to check meats for doneness. Common safe internal temperatures are as follows:

Breads and cakes	210°F	(99°C)
Baked potatoes	205°F	(96°C)
Chicken thighs and wings	180°F	(82°C)
Beef (well-done)	165°F	(74°C)
Chicken breasts	165°F	(74°C)
Ground beef	155°F	(68°C)
Pork	145°F	(63°C)

Mason jars. Wide-mouth mason jars are the perfect size to fit an immersion blender. You can fit up to four tall pint-size (473 ml) wide-mouth mason jars in a 6-quart (5.7 L) pressure cooker, allowing you to cook multiple foods at the same time. (Be aware that common brands make two shapes of pint-size [473 ml] wide-mouth mason jars—short and tall—and only the tall ones fit four at once.)

Retriever tongs. Many people prefer to use these little grabbers to remove the inner pan from the pressure cooking pot when doing pot-in-pot cooking.

Round cake pan. A 7 x 3-inch (18 x 7.5 cm) round cake pan is a pressure cooking must! It's the secret for pot-in-pot cooking, which allows you to cook sides and sauces at the same time you cook your meal. If you wish to make the smash cakes in chapter 5, you'll also need a 4 x 2-inch (10 x 5 cm) round cake pan.

Silicone baby food containers. These flexible containers are perfect for making mini muffins and egg bites. The recipes in this book are developed for an 8-inch (20 cm) tray with seven cups. The flexible silicone makes it easy to remove the cooked foods from the cups with a gentle push on the bottom of the cup.

Silicone mini mitts. These inexpensive, flexible mitts work like hot pads but give you more grip and control when handling a hot pressure cooking pot—and the all-silicone design is extra easy to clean.

Sling. A sling makes it much easier to remove hot pans from the cooking pot when doing pot-in-pot cooking. You can make your own sling out of a long strip of aluminum foil folded into thirds so it's about 26 inches (66 cm) long by 4 inches (10 cm) wide.

Springform pan. We recommend a leakproof 7-inch (18 cm) springform pan for making foods that may be hard to remove from a cake pan, such as Alex's Brownie Pops (page 170).

Steamer basket. A steamer basket keeps foods out of the water and has small holes like a colander. This tool is really useful for cooking foods that break down easily in water and makes them easy to remove from the pressure cooking pot.

Trivet. A trivet (sometimes called a rack) keeps ingredients and pots off the bottom of the pressure cooking pot. Because they are relatively inexpensive, we prefer to have two:

a short trivet (½ inch [1.3 cm] or less) for taller cooking accessories like mason jars and a tall trivet (2 to 3 inches [5 to 7.5 cm] high) for cooking side dishes and sauces over a main dish.

Tips, Tricks, and Troubleshooting

Life with babies and toddlers is busy enough—the last thing you need is to spend time running to the store in the middle of cooking or trying to fix a meal that didn't work out. Here are a few tips and tricks that will help you get started.

Know your model size. The recipes in this cookbook were created in and tested using a 6-quart (5.7 L) electric pressure cooker. While these recipes will work in larger pressure cookers, your cook time may be slightly different, and you may need to use more liquid than the recipe calls for. Many of the recipes will also work in smaller pressure cookers; however, some of the pot-in-pot recipes may need to have the main and side dishes cooked separately.

Read the whole recipe before you start cooking. This is a simple thing that has a huge effect on your cooking (and your stress level while cooking)! Reading though the recipe ensures you're familiar with the timing and ingredients, accounts for any resting time, and helps reduce errors. Also, many recipes have serving suggestions at the end, so reading ahead helps you plan when you need to start these items so they'll be ready when you need them.

Prepare your ingredients before cooking. It's frustrating to get halfway through a recipe and realize you're missing a key ingredient. By having your ingredients measured and chopped before you start cooking, you'll be ready for quick transitions and the actual cooking process will go more smoothly.

Trust your senses. Listen to your intuition and don't doubt what you see and smell! For example, if the recipe calls for more time, but the food you're cooking looks and smells done, then move on to the next step. If the food looks or smells like it's cooking too quickly, take the cooking pot out of the housing or add the liquid to the pot.

Check the temperature of your meat. Due to variations in size and thickness, sometimes the meat in your pot will need a little longer cook time than the recipe suggests. As soon as you've released the pressure, you'll want to check the meat for doneness, consulting the temperature guidelines on page 25.

Grease your pans generously. When you spray your pans with nonstick cooking or baking spray, make sure you're using enough to coat the pans well and that you're spreading it around well with a paper towel, distributing the spray along any corners or creases. (This is especially important with the silicone pans, where foods are more likely to stick.)

Get familiar with pot-in-pot cooking. When you're cooking pot-in-pot, some foods may take a little longer to cook because they're a little farther from the heating element. (For example, we've found white rice does better with 4 minutes pot-in-pot, compared to 3 minutes when cooked the traditional way.) If something you've cooked pot-in-pot isn't done to your liking, make a note to add another minute or two the next time you make it. Also, if you're steaming something pot-in-pot, try to get in the habit of adding the water to the cooking pot *before* you put the trivet or steamer basket in place—just to make sure you don't forget it!

Cook a double batch of favorite recipes. Many of these recipes are easily doubled in a standard 6-quart (5.7 L) pressure cooker without increasing the cook time. However, be aware that if you're doubling a main dish, it may be too much volume to cook the side pot-in-pot at the same time.

Follow food safety practices. This includes basics like washing your hands well, keeping raw meats away from other food prep, and thawing food in the refrigerator or in cold water. Cooked food must be refrigerated or frozen within 2 hours or discarded, and the sooner you can get leftovers in the fridge, the better. Once refrigerated, be sure to use or freeze according to USDA or common food standards. (And, of course, use your judgment—when in doubt, throw it out!)

COOKED FOOD		
	Refrigerator	**Freezer**
Baked goods (muffins, brownies)	3-5 days	2-3 months
Beef	3-4 days	2-3 months*
Chicken	3-4 days	2-3 months*
Cut fruits	3-4 days	1-2 months
Fruit sauces (compotes)	Up to 7 days	2-3 months
Pasta	3-5 days	1-2 months
Pork	3-4 days	2-3 months*
Potatoes	3-4 days	1-2 months
Rice	4-6 days	4-6 months
Soups	3-4 days	2-3 months
Vegetables	3-4 day	1-2 months

* If meats are covered in gravy or broth, they can be stored in the freezer for up to 6 months.

Solutions to Common Concerns

Once in a while, something goes wrong as you're cooking—it even happens to cooks who aren't distracted by children! For brand-specific troubleshooting tips, consult your pressure cooker user manual; however, for your convenience we've included our solutions to the most common concerns we hear from blog readers, family, and friends.

Steam is coming from my pressure cooker. First, determine where the steam is coming from. If it's coming from the pressure release switch or the float valve, double-check that the pressure release switch is fully in place and turned to the Sealed position. If it's from the float valve, use a quick pressure release and remove the lid, then check that the float valve is properly installed and that the mini gasket is tightly in place. If steam is escaping from the sides of the lid, use a quick pressure release and check that the silicone sealing ring is tightly in place around the entire lid. In rare cases, the sealing ring may be cracked or broken; in this case, unfortunately, the only solution is to replace it.

If you notice the steam escaping early in the cooking process, you can simply restart the High Pressure cook time. However, if a number of minutes went by before you noticed the problem, you may need to add more liquid to the cooking pot and reduce the cook time—there's no hard rule for how much, just make your best guess.

My pressure cooker sprays liquid when releasing the steam. This can happen, especially when you're cooking starchy foods like grains, dried beans, or pastas. If water starts to spray during your quick pressure release, return the pressure release switch to the Sealed position. Wait 30 seconds, then open the pressure release switch again and allow pressure to release. If more liquid comes out, repeat the process. With some foods, one or two closed intervals is all you need before you can leave the switch in the Venting position; with other foods, it takes several closed intervals to fully release the pressure.

My food scorched while using the Sauté setting. Be aware that the sauté times in the recipes are guidelines; due to differences in thickness and sizes of meats and vegetables, your food may need more or less time. If your food needs less time browning, simply add the premeasured liquid called for in the recipes (often broth or water). If your food needs additional time browning, if needed, simply add another tablespoon (15 ml) of oil or butter and continue the cooking process.

Also, just like a pot on an electric stovetop, you can also lift the cooking pot away from the heating element in the housing to slow the cooking process. If possible, adjust your pressure cooker to sauté on a lower heat setting. (If your pressure cooker does not adjust to low, consider browning in a separate pot on the stove.) Finally, if you're cooking pot-in-pot, make sure the inside pot is resting on a trivet above liquids and not directly on the pressure cooking pot.

My food isn't cooked through. If your food is nearly done, select Sauté and finish cooking the dish on that setting for a few minutes. However, if your meat isn't close to the proper temperature or isn't as fall-apart tender as you'd like, lock the lid in place and cook for a few additional minutes at High Pressure, then use the pressure release called for in the recipe. If quicker-cooking foods like vegetables or rice are done but your meat is not, if possible, remove these ingredients from the cooking pot and cover them with aluminum foil before returning the meat to High Pressure.

If this happens when you're "baking" foods in the pressure cooker, make sure you've followed the instructions on whether to bake covered or uncovered, since covering the pan with foil has a big effect on the total cook time.

My food stuck to the pan. If you're cooking pot-in-pot, spray your inner pan generously with nonstick cooking spray or baking spray with flour and use a paper towel to ensure the entire pan is coated. Let your food cool in the pan for at least 5 minutes before trying to remove the lid; if necessary, run a thin spatula around the edges of the pan to help separate it.

If your food stuck to the pressure cooking pot, make sure that you added enough liquid and that it was evenly distributed on the bottom of the cooking pot. Since the bottom of the cooking pot is slightly domed, the melted butter and oil tend to run to the sides—in these instances, tilt the cooking pot so that the oil covers the entire surface. Finally, remember that larger 8- and 10-quart (7.6 to 9.5 L) cookers may need more liquid than their smaller 6-quart (5.7 L) counter-parts.

My soup/sauce/compote/oatmeal/risotto turned out too thin. When these foods come out of the pressure cooker too thin, there's usually an easy fix. First, give the ingredients a good stir to ensure that the liquid hasn't settled on the top. Next, remember that these foods thicken as they cool, so if they're close to your desired thickness, remove the cooking pot from the housing, allow to cool uncovered for 5 minutes, then check the thickness again. If there's much more liquid than desired, select Sauté and cook, stirring constantly, until the food reaches the desired thickness.

If you're in a hurry, you can also add a thickener to soups, sauces, and compotes. In a small bowl, stir together 1 tablespoon (8 g) cornstarch and 1 tablespoon (15 ml) cold water and slowly add the slurry to the cooking pot, stirring constantly. Select Sauté and stir until the food reaches a boiling point, which will activate the thickening agents in the cornstarch. (When in doubt, take a lighter hand on the thickener because too much can create a gelatin effect.)

My soup/sauce/compote/oatmeal/risotto turned out too thick. If your foods come out of the pressure cooker too thick, you'll need to give them a good stir to ensure nothing has scorched on the bottom. If not, simply add more of the main liquid in the recipe (e.g., water, broth, cream, juice, almond milk) and stir until well combined. You'll often need to add a good amount of liquids when reheating leftovers, because these foods thicken significantly as they cool.

My food isn't sweet/spicy/flavorful enough. Keep in mind that these recipes were designed for the toddler palate and that adults are welcome to add favorite seasonings or extra sugar to adjust the meal to their individual tastes. Also, for meals that call for fruits, there can be a big variation in the sweetness and ripeness of the fruits, so you'll want to taste it before cooking. If the fruit is very tart, add a little sugar or juice before cooking.

My silicone ring still smells like yesterday's dinner. Unfortunately, the food-grade silicone that allows pressure cookers to come to pressure also has a tendency to take on the smells of the foods being cooked—we haven't yet come across a brand of pressure cooker that doesn't have this problem. For the most part, the odor will not impact the food you're cooking.

Although there are dozens of methods that try to remove food smells from the silicone ring—soaking or steaming in lemon juice, vinegar, coffee grounds, tomato juice, and even bleach—we haven't found one that completely gets rid of the smell. To minimize the smell, we prefer to store the silicone rings so they have a chance to air out and to have one ring for savory meats and another for mild breakfast foods and desserts.

Part

one

Baby Food

Chapter 1

First Fruits and Vegetables

When introducing babies to solid foods, pediatricians recommend starting with just one new food at a time. Single-ingredient fruits and vegetables are gentle and great for baby's first solids. Plus, these made-fresh purees look and taste so much better than commercial first foods—you may find yourself eating some of them along with your baby.

Recipes

Apple Puree

Apples are naturally sweet and are loaded with vitamins and fiber. They would make a delicious choice for introducing your baby to fruits.

MAKES 3½ CUPS (820 ML).

5 large soft apples (such as Jonagold, Fuji, or Golden Delicious), peeled, cored, and quartered

¼ cup (60 ml) water

1 Place the apple quarters and water in the pressure cooking pot. Lock the lid in place. Select High Pressure and 4 minutes cook time.

2 When the cook time ends, turn off the pressure cooker. Let the pressure release naturally for 5 minutes, then finish with a quick pressure release. When the float valve drops, carefully remove the lid. Allow to cool for 20 minutes.

3 Transfer the contents of the cooking pot to a blender jar or food processer and blend until very smooth. (Add water if needed to blend but use the minimum amount necessary.)

Tip

This recipe calls for peeled apples since apple skins have extra fiber, which can affect babies' sensitive tummies. Once your baby is a little older and ready for more texture in foods, you can skip peeling the apples if you prefer.

Dried Apricot Puree

If your baby isn't a fan of prunes, dried apricots have a similar effect with a very different, sweet-tart taste. By using dried, you never have to worry about whether your apricots will be ripe or sweet enough.

MAKES 1½ TO 2 CUPS (355 TO 475 ML).

1 cup (130 g) dried apricots, approximately 25
1¾ cups (410 ml) water

1 In the pressure cooking pot, add the dried apricots and water. Stir to ensure the dried apricots are completely submerged. Lock the lid in place. Select High Pressure and 10 minutes cook time.

2 When the cook time ends, turn off the pressure cooking pot. Let the pressure release naturally for 10 minutes, then finish with a quick pressure release. When the float valve drops, carefully remove the lid.

3 Use a slotted spoon to remove the dried apricots from the pressure cooking pot, reserving the cooking water. Allow to cool for 20 minutes.

4 Place the cooked apricots in a blender jar or food processer and add 1 cup (235 ml) reserved cooking water. Blend until very smooth. (Add more water if needed to blend but use the minimum amount necessary.)

Tip

Check the packaging label and avoid buying dried apricots with sulfates, added sugars, artificial colors, or preservatives.

Dried Plum (Prune) Puree

Whether the label calls them "dried plums" or "prunes," these little fruits are the go-to food for keeping baby regular.

MAKES 1½ TO 2 CUPS (355 TO 475 ML).

1 cup (175 g) dried plums, approximately 25

1¾ cups (410 ml) water

1 In the pressure cooking pot, add the dried plums and water. Stir to ensure the plums are completely submerged. Lock the lid in place. Select High Pressure and 10 minutes cook time.

2 When the cook time ends, turn off the pressure cooker. Let the pressure release naturally for 10 minutes, then finish with a quick pressure release. When the float valve drops, carefully remove the lid.

3 Use a slotted spoon to remove the dried plums from the pressure cooking pot, reserving the cooking water. Allow to cool for 20 minutes.

4 Place the cooked plums in a blender jar or food processer and add 1 cup (235 ml) reserved cooking water. Blend until very smooth. (Add more water if needed to blend but use the minimum amount necessary.)

Tip

If your baby isn't a fan of prune puree, try mixing it with other fruit purees, such as Apple Puree (page 34). If your baby still won't take it, try the Dried Apricot Puree (page 35).

Nectarine Puree

We prefer nectarines to peaches just because we don't have to bother with the skins. With this recipe, you can blend the puree with the skins on.

MAKES 3 TO 4 CUPS (700 TO 946 ML).

8 large nectarines, halved and pitted

1 Place a steamer basket in the bottom of the pressure cooking pot and add 1 cup (235 ml) water. Place the nectarines inside the basket and lock the lid in place. Select High Pressure and 5 minutes cook time.

2 When the cook time ends, turn off the pressure cooker. Let the pressure release naturally for 10 minutes, then finish with a quick pressure release. When the float valve drops, carefully remove the lid.

3 Remove the nectarines from the pressure cooking pot, reserving the cooking water. Allow to cool until comfortable to handle.

4 Place the steamed nectarines in a blender jar or food processer with 1 cup (235 ml) reserved cooking water. Blend until very smooth. (Very juicy nectarines will require less liquid. Add reserved cooking water if needed to blend but use the minimum amount necessary.)

Tip

When selecting nectarines, pick fruit that has a slight give. Nectarines are very easy to halve when they're ripe, but you may still need to use a knife to cut around the pit to remove it. If your nectarines aren't quite ripe enough, place them in a paper bag for a day or two to ripen.

Peach Puree

You can use white or yellow peaches with this recipe—white peaches are a little sweeter and less tart, while yellow peaches will result in a traditional golden puree.

MAKES 3 TO 4 CUPS (700 TO 946 ML).

8 large peaches, halved and pitted

1 Place a steamer basket in the bottom of the pressure cooking pot and add 1 cup (235 ml) water. Place the peaches inside the basket and lock the lid in place. Select High Pressure and 5 minutes cook time.

2 When the cook time ends, turn off the pressure cooker. Let the pressure release naturally for 10 minutes, then finish with a quick pressure release. When the float valve drops, carefully remove the lid.

3 Remove the peaches from the cooking pot, reserving the cooking water. Allow to cool until comfortable to handle, then peel off the skins.

4 Place the steamed peaches in a blender jar or food processer and blend until very smooth. (Add reserved cooking water if needed to blend but use the minimum amount necessary. Very juicy peaches won't require any additional liquid; less ripe peaches may need up to ½ cup (120 ml).)

Tip

If you're using frozen peaches, use a 0-minute cook time and a quick pressure release. If your pressure cooker doesn't allow you to set your cook time for 0 minutes, set your pressure cooker for the minimum time possible and release the pressure as soon as the machine reaches pressure.

Pear Puree

Pears are a terrific first fruit for baby. Bartlett pears are a good choice for pear puree because they are soft, mild, and sweet, but you can use this recipe with any variety of pear.

MAKES 3 TO 4 CUPS (700 TO 946 ML).

5 large pears, peeled, cored, and quartered

½ cup (120 ml) water

1 Place the pear quarters and water in the pressure cooking pot. Lock the lid in place. Select High Pressure and 4 minutes cook time.

2 When the cook time ends, turn off the pressure cooker. Let the pressure release naturally for 5 minutes, then finish with a quick pressure release. When the float valve drops, carefully remove the lid. Allow to cool for 20 minutes.

3 Transfer the contents of the cooking pot to a blender jar or food processer and blend until very smooth. (Add water if needed to blend but use the minimum amount necessary.)

Tip

If your pears aren't sweet, you can substitute apple juice for the water. If your pears are very ripe, you may not need to cook them as long (or at all)—just puree them in a blender and serve.

Butternut Squash Puree

There's no need to remove the rind before you pressure cook! After pressure cooking, the softened rind is easy to cut away.

MAKES 5 TO 6 CUPS (1.2 TO 1.4 L).

1 fresh butternut squash

1 Wash the butternut squash. Do not peel. Use a sharp knife to remove the ends, then cut the neck away from the body, and slice the neck into quarters. Cut the body in half and use a spoon to scrape out the seeds and stringy flesh. Cut each half of the body into quarters.

2 Place a trivet in the bottom of the pressure cooking pot and add 1 cup (235 ml) water. Carefully stack the butternut squash pieces on top. Lock the lid in place. Select High Pressure and 5 minutes cook time.

3 When the cook time ends, turn off the pressure cooker. Let the pressure release naturally for 10 minutes, then finish with a quick pressure release. When the float valve drops, carefully remove the lid.

4 Remove the butternut squash from the cooking pot, reserving the cooking water. Allow to cool until comfortable to handle.

5 Use a knife to remove the rind from the butternut squash pieces and place the flesh in a blender jar or food processer. Add ½ cup (120 ml) reserved cooking water and blend until very smooth. (Add more water if needed to blend but use the minimum amount necessary.)

Tip

If you want to skip removing the rind, many grocery and warehouse stores sell pre-packaged fresh or frozen cubed butternut squash. Some stores sell the butternut squash in large 2-inch (5 cm) pieces; others come in much smaller ½-inch (1.3 cm) pieces. Place 1 cup (235 ml) water and a steamer basket in the bottom of the pressure cooking pot. Place 2 cups (280 g) frozen butternut squash chunks inside the basket. The cook time will depend on the size—for larger pieces, cook for 4 minutes; for smaller pieces, cook for 2 to 3 minutes. This yields about 1½ cups (210 g) squash.

Carrot Puree

Carrots are easy to digest and packed with fiber and antioxidants like vitamin A. Steaming carrots makes the nutrients even easier to digest, and their sweet flavor often makes them a hit with new eaters.

MAKES 2 TO 3 CUPS (475 ML TO 700 ML).

8 fresh carrots, peeled and cut into approximately 2-inch (5 cm) pieces

1 Place a steamer basket in the bottom of the pressure cooking pot and add 1 cup (235 ml) water. Place the carrots inside the basket. Lock the lid in place. Select High Pressure and 4 minutes cook time.

2 When the cook time ends, turn off the pressure cooker. Let the pressure release naturally for 10 minutes, then finish with a quick pressure release. When the float valve drops carefully remove the lid.

3 Remove the carrots from the steamer basket, reserving the cooking water. Allow to cool for 20 minutes.

4 Place the steamed carrots in a blender jar or food processer. Add ¾ cup (175 ml) reserved cooking water and blend until very smooth. (Add more water if needed to blend but use the minimum amount necessary.)

Tip

If you're in a hurry, you can use prepackaged peeled carrots, baby carrots, or frozen carrots. If you're using frozen carrots, use 2 cups (260 g) frozen carrots, a 3-minute cook time, and a quick pressure release.

Green Bean Puree

Rich in vitamin A and fiber, green beans are a nutritious addition to a baby's diet.

MAKES 1½ CUPS (355 ML).

4 cups (400 g) fresh green beans, ends trimmed

1 Place a steamer basket in the bottom of the pressure cooking pot and add 1 cup (235 ml) water. Place the green beans inside the basket. Lock the lid in place. Select High Pressure and 4 minutes cook time.

2 When the cook time ends, turn off the pressure cooker. Let the pressure release naturally for 10 minutes, then finish with a quick pressure release. When the float valve drops, carefully remove the lid.

3 Remove the green beans from the steamer basket, reserving the cooking water. Allow to cool for 20 minutes.

4 Place the steamed green beans in a blender jar or food processer. Add ½ cup (120 ml) reserved cooking water and blend until very smooth. (Add more water if needed to blend but use the minimum amount necessary.)

Tip

Frozen fruits and vegetables are often picked at the peak of freshness, so they are a great option for making baby foods. We often prefer using frozen green beans to skip washing and trimming. If you're using frozen green beans, use 3 cups (372 g) frozen green beans, a 3-minute cook time, and a quick pressure release.

Pea Puree

Peas make a wonderful first green vegetable for baby—they're on the sweeter side, a good source of fiber, and have a bright green color. Because frozen peas are already shelled and taste great year-round, we generally cook from frozen; however, you can make purees with fresh shelled peas with no change to the cook time.

MAKES 1½ CUPS (355 ML).

2 cups shelled peas (300 g), fresh or (260 g) frozen

1 Place a steamer basket in the bottom of the pressure cooking pot and add 1 cup (235 ml) water. Place the peas inside the basket. Lock the lid in place. Select High Pressure and 2 minutes cook time.

2 When the cook time ends, turn off the pressure cooker. Use a quick pressure release. When the float valve drops, carefully remove the lid.

3 Remove the peas from the steamer basket, reserving the cooking water. Allow to cool for 20 minutes.

4 Place the steamed peas in a blender jar or food processor. Add ¾ cup (175 ml) reserved cooking water and blend until very smooth. (Add more water if needed to blend but use the minimum amount necessary.)

Tip

Sometimes the outer "skin" of the peas won't puree smooth; if you wish to remove them from the puree before serving, pass them through a fine-mesh sieve.

Spaghetti Squash Puree

This squash is easy to cook in the pressure cooker. It has a mild flavor and a beautiful golden color when pureed.

MAKES ABOUT 4 CUPS (946 ML).

1 fresh spaghetti squash (about 2 pounds, or 900 g)

1 Wash the spaghetti squash. Do not peel. Use a sharp knife to remove the stem end of the squash, then cut the squash in half vertically, and remove the seeds with a spoon.

2 Place a trivet in the bottom of the pressure cooking pot and add 1 cup (235 ml) water. Carefully place the spaghetti squash pieces on top. Lock the lid in place. Select High Pressure and 8 minutes cook time.

3 When the cook time ends, turn off the pressure cooker. Let the pressure release naturally for 2 minutes, then finish with a quick pressure release. When the float valve drops, carefully remove the lid.

4 Remove the spaghetti squash from the cooking pot, reserving the cooking water. Allow to cool until comfortable to handle, then remove the skin.

5 Place the flesh in a blender jar or food processer. Add ¾ cup (175 ml) reserved cooking water and blend until very smooth. (Add more water if needed to blend but use the minimum amount necessary.)

Tip

When baby is a bit bigger, rather than making a puree, serve this squash as a replacement spaghetti. Cool until comfortable to handle, then use a fork to scrape the strands of "spaghetti" from the skin. We like to serve this when the adults are eating spaghetti—mix the spaghetti squash, some spaghetti pieces, and a little sauce.

Sweet Potato Puree

Here are two ways for your baby to enjoy nutritious sweet potato: one for when they are just getting started with solid foods, and one for when they are ready for a sweet but healthy treat.

MAKES 3 TO 4 CUPS (700 TO 946 ML).

2 large sweet potatoes

1 Peel the sweet potatoes. Cut in half lengthwise and cut into ¼ -inch (6 mm) slices. Place a trivet in the bottom of the pressure cooking pot and add 1 cup (235 ml) water. Place the sweet potato slices on the trivet. Lock the lid in place. Select High Pressure and 15 minutes cook time.

2 When the cook time ends, turn off the pressure cooker. Let the pressure release naturally for 10 minutes, then finish with a quick pressure release. When the float valve drops, carefully remove the lid.

3 Remove the sweet potatoes from the pressure cooking pot, reserving the cooking water. Allow to cool for 20 minutes.

4 Place the cooled sweet potatoes in a blender jar or food processer and add ½ to ¾ cup (120 to 175 ml) reserved cooking water. Blend until very smooth. (Add more water if needed to blend but use the minimum amount necessary to get to your preferred consistency.)

Dessert Variation

1 tablespoon (15 g) brown sugar

1 tablespoon (14 g) unsalted butter, melted

¼ teaspoon vanilla extract

¼ teaspoon ground cinnamon

1 tablespoon (15 ml) heavy cream

Pressure cook the sweet potatoes as directed above. When ready to blend, add ½ cup (120 ml) reserved cooking water and the brown sugar, butter, vanilla, and cinnamon, and blend until smooth. Add the heavy cream and mix well.

Tip

For this recipe, you'll want to buy the soft sweet potatoes, which have copper skin and orange flesh.

4-in-1-Pot Single-Ingredient Purees

This easy recipe shows you how to make four different purees at the same time—and you can even blend them in the jars they cook in!

MAKES FOUR 1-CUP (235 ML) SERVINGS.

1 to 2 fresh peaches, peeled, pitted, and diced
1 to 2 fresh apples, peeled, cored, and diced
1 to 2 fresh pears, peeled, cored and diced
1½ cups (210 g) frozen diced butternut squash

1 Add each ingredient to one of four separate wide-mouth pint-size (473 ml) mason jars. Use as much as will fit in the jar, but do not overfill. Do not place lids on the mason jars.

2 Add 1 cup (235 ml) water to the pressure cooking pot. Add a trivet to the pot and place the mason jars on top. Lock the lid in place. Select High Pressure and 6 minutes cook time.

3 When the cook time ends, turn off the pressure cooker. Let the pressure release naturally for 5 minutes, then finish with a quick pressure release. When the float valve drops, carefully remove the lid.

4 Remove the mason jars from the pressure cooking pot. Allow to cool for 20 minutes, then use an immersion blender directly in the mason jars to puree to your desired consistency.

Tip

This process can be adapted for many different foods. You need to choose recipes that have similar cook times and cooking needs. For example, most frozen fruits and vegetables cook with steam, have similar cook times, and use a short pressure release, so they would work well together. Foods like dried plums that need to cook directly in water would not be a good fit for this process. Because the mason jars shield ingredients from the heat, you may need to increase the cook time by 25 to 50 percent of what was listed in the original recipe. (For example, the apples cook for 4 minutes in the Apple Puree [page 34], but need 6 minutes when cooked inside the mason jar.)

Chapter 2

Grains and Legumes

Homemade grain and legume purees are generally not as smooth as commercial cereals, so take that into consideration as you decide when your baby is ready for grains. We've listed the recipes in the order we prefer to introduce them—oats, corn, rice, wheat, quinoa, then legumes; however, use the order that works best for your baby. Since babies eat very small amounts at first, one small batch of grains will last a long time. We like to make a batch and refrigerate enough for a day or two, then freeze the rest in individual portions to combine with fruit or meat purees.

Recipes

Rolled Oats

Rolled oats are a wonderful first grain! Once baby is ready for grains, we love to mix these oats with an apple puree. When they're ready for spices, add a little ground cinnamon and this cereal is sure to be a favorite.

MAKES 1½ cups (351 G).

½ cup (40 g) old-fashioned rolled oats
1 cup (235 ml) water

1 Place a trivet in the bottom of the pressure cooking pot and add 1 cup (235 ml) water.

2 In a 7-inch (18 cm) cake pan, stir together the oats and 1 cup (235 ml) water. Use a sling to lower the pan carefully onto the trivet. Lock the lid in place. Select High Pressure and 2 minutes cook time.

3 When the cook time ends, turn off the pressure cooker.

Let the pressure release naturally for 5 minutes, then finish with a quick pressure release. When the float valve drops, carefully remove the lid. Use the sling to remove the pan from the pressure cooking pot and allow to cool for 20 minutes.

4 Transfer the cooled oats to a bowl. For younger eaters, use a baby food mill to puree until smooth.

Tip

Be sure to avoid using instant or quick oats in this recipe. Instant and quick oats are rolled thinner and chopped more finely, so they cook too quickly for the pressure cooker.

Steel Cut Oats

Steel cut oats are the least processed form of oats with the lowest glycemic index. They also cook up a bit chunkier than rolled oats and have a nuttier flavor, which makes them perfect once baby is ready for some texture.

MAKES 1½ cups (351 G).

½ cup (40 g) steel cut oats, rinsed
2 cups (475 ml) water

1 Place a trivet in the bottom of the pressure cooking pot and add 1 cup (235 ml) water.

2 In a 7-inch (18 cm) cake pan, stir together the oats and 2 cups (475 ml) water. Use a sling to lower the pan carefully onto the trivet. Lock the lid in place. Select High Pressure and 14 minutes cook time.

3 When the cook time ends, turn off the pressure cooker. Let the pressure release naturally for 12 minutes, then finish with a quick pressure release. When the float valve drops, carefully remove the lid.

4 Use the sling to remove the pan from the pressure cooking pot and fluff the oats with a fork. Allow to cool for 20 minutes.

5 Transfer the cooled oats to a bowl. For younger eaters, use a baby food mill to puree until smooth.

Tip

Steel cut oats are a blank slate—they pair well with pretty much any fruit puree or diced fruit, and the hearty oats help your baby stay full.

Polenta (Corn)

Since polenta is made from ground cornmeal, it is a fantastic first baby food for those concerned about gluten. Making polenta in the pressure cooker is so much easier than making it on the stovetop!

MAKES 1½ cups (235 G).

½ cup (70 g) coarse polenta
1 cup (235 ml) water

1 Place a trivet in the bottom of the pressure cooking pot and add 1 cup (235 ml) water.

2 In a 7-inch (18 cm) cake pan, combine the polenta and 1 cup (235 ml) water and stir to ensure the polenta is completely submerged. Use a sling to lower the pan carefully onto the trivet. Lock the lid in place. Select High Pressure and 5 minutes cook time.

3 When the cook time ends, turn off the pressure cooker.

Let the pressure release naturally for 10 minutes, then finish with a quick pressure release. When the float valve drops, carefully remove the lid.

4 Use the sling to remove the pan from the pressure cooking pot and fluff the polenta with a fork. Allow to cool for 20 minutes.

5 Serve as prepared or mix with vegetable, meat, or fruit purees.

Tip

If you prefer a smoother texture, you can swap grits for the polenta since both are made from different varieties of dried corn. Traditionally, polenta is made from yellow corn and has a coarser texture, while grits are generally made from white corn and have a finer texture. However, read the labels carefully and avoid polenta or grits that are "quick-cooking" or "instant."

White Rice

Rice cereal has been a classic first food for generations because it's gentle on baby's tummy and unlikely to cause any food sensitivities. The mild flavor makes it easy to introduce to babies.

MAKES 1½ CUPS (275 G).

½ cup (93 g) long-grain white rice, rinsed

⅔ cup (160 ml) water

1 Place a trivet in the bottom of the pressure cooking pot and add 1 cup (235 ml) water.

2 In a 7-inch (18 cm) cake pan, combine the rice and ⅔ cup (160 ml) water and stir to ensure the rice is completely submerged. Use a sling to lower the pan carefully onto the trivet. Lock the lid in place. Select High Pressure and 4 minutes cook time.

3 When the cook time ends, turn off the pressure cooker. Let the pressure release naturally for 7 minutes, then finish with a quick pressure release. When the float valve drops, carefully remove the lid.

4 Use the sling to remove the pan from the pressure cooking pot and fluff the rice with a fork. Allow to cool for 20 minutes.

5 For younger eaters, use a baby food mill to puree until smooth. For older eaters, serve as a finger food or mix with a vegetable, meat, or fruit puree.

Tip

To make the rice cook up less sticky, use a hot water rinse and soak. Place the rice in a fine-mesh strainer and rinse well with hot water until the water runs clear. Place the rice in a bowl of hot water and let sit for 30 minutes. Pour the rice back into a fine-mesh strainer and rinse to remove any remaining starch. Continue with the recipe as directed.

Brown Rice

Brown rice and white rice come from the same grain, but brown rice is much higher in B vitamins and fiber, thanks to the bran outer coating. Brown rice lets your baby experience a new, chewy texture and nutty flavor.

MAKES 1½ cups (275 G).

½ cup (93 g) long-grain brown rice, rinsed

¾ cup (175 ml) water

1 Place a trivet in the bottom of the pressure cooking pot and add 1 cup (235 ml) water.

2 In a 7-inch (18 cm) cake pan, combine the rice and ¾ cup (175 ml) water and stir to ensure the rice is completely submerged. Use a sling to lower the pan carefully onto the trivet. Lock the lid in place. Select High Pressure and 27 minutes cook time.

3 When the cook time ends, turn off the pressure cooker. Let the pressure release naturally for 10 minutes, then finish with a quick pressure release. When the float valve drops, carefully remove the lid.

4 Use the sling to remove the pan from the pressure cooking pot and fluff the rice with a fork. Allow to cool for 20 minutes.

5 For younger eaters, use a baby food mill to puree until smooth. For older eaters, serve as a finger food or mix with a vegetable, meat, or fruit puree.

Tip

To freeze, divide the rice into individual servings using silicone baby food trays. Once frozen, remove the rice from the trays and store in a ziplock bag.

Farro (Wheat)

Farro is an ancient whole grain, and it's lower in gluten than many other wheat varieties, which makes it an excellent way to introduce wheat to your baby's diet.

MAKES 1½ cups (237 G).

½ cup (104 g) pearled or semi-pearled farro
1 cups (235 ml) water

1 Place a trivet in the bottom of the pressure cooking pot and add 1 cup (235 ml) water.

2 In a 7-inch (18 cm) cake pan, combine the farro and 1 cup (235 ml) water and stir to ensure the farro is completely submerged. Use a sling to lower the pan carefully onto the trivet. Lock the lid in place. Select High Pressure and 20 minutes cook time.

3 When the cook time ends, turn off the pressure cooker. Let the pressure release naturally for 10 minutes, then finish with a quick pressure release. When the float valve drops, carefully remove the lid.

4 Use the sling to remove the pan from the pressure cooking pot and fluff the farro with a fork. Allow to cool for 20 minutes.

5 For younger eaters, use a baby food mill to puree until smooth. For older eaters, serve as a finger food or mix with a vegetable, meat, or fruit puree.

Tip

The cook time for farro varies significantly depending on the type of farro grain used, and sometimes, it can be hard to tell what kind of farro your store sells. When in doubt, check the cook time on your package. The whole-grain farro generally has a cook time around 30 to 40 minutes and needs an overnight soak. Semi-pearled and pearled farro have part or all of the bran removed and have a shorter cook time, around 15 to 25 minutes.

Couscous (Wheat)

Couscous is made from semolina wheat and is an excellent stand-in for pasta in baby food recipes. These chewy yet firm balls are wonderful to eat on their own and even better when mixed with purees.

MAKES 1½ CUPS (236 G).

½ cup (86 g) pearl couscous, rinsed
⅔ cup (395 ml) water

1 Place a trivet in the bottom of the pressure cooking pot and add 1 cup (235 ml) water.

2 In a 7-inch (18 cm) cake pan, combine the couscous and ⅔ cup (160 ml) water and stir to ensure the couscous is completely submerged. Use a sling to lower the pan carefully onto the trivet. Lock the lid in place. Select High Pressure and 8 minutes cook time.

3 When the cook time ends, turn off the pressure cooker. Let the pressure release naturally for 2 minutes, then finish with a quick pressure release. When the float valve drops, carefully remove the lid.

4 Use the sling to remove the pan from the pressure cooking pot and fluff the couscous with a fork. Allow to cool for 20 minutes.

5 For younger eaters, use a baby food mill to puree until smooth. For older eaters, serve as a finger food or mix with a vegetable, meat, or fruit puree.

Tip

Couscous comes in a variety of sizes. We prefer the larger pearl couscous; however, if you've purchased a smaller variety like Moroccan couscous, reduce the cook time to 2 minutes.

Quinoa

Quinoa is a gluten-free seed that's also a nutritional powerhouse! Packing lots of protein and iron, all nine amino acids, and lots of fiber, it's a perfect addition to your baby's diet.

MAKES 1½ CUPS (278 G).

½ cup (87 g) quinoa, well rinsed
½ cup (120 ml) water

1 Place a trivet in the bottom of the pressure cooking pot and add 1 cup (235 ml) water.

2 In a 7-inch (18 cm) cake pan, combine the quinoa and ½ cup (120 ml) water and stir to ensure the quinoa is completely submerged. Use a sling to lower the pan carefully onto the trivet. Lock the lid in place. Select High Pressure and 4 minutes cook time.

3 When the cook time ends, turn off the pressure cooker. Let the pressure release naturally for 10 minutes, then finish with a quick pressure release. When the float valve drops, carefully remove the lid.

4 Use the sling to remove the pan from the pressure cooking pot and fluff the quinoa with a fork. Allow to cool for 20 minutes.

5 Serve as prepared or mix with vegetable, meat, or fruit purees.

Tip

Even though most quinoa comes pre-rinsed, we still prefer to give it a good rinse in a fine-mesh strainer until the water runs clear, just to avoid any bitter taste once cooked.

Black Beans

With their dark color, soft texture, and easy-to-pick-up size, well-cooked black beans make an excellent finger food for babies.

MAKES 2 CUPS (370 G).

1 cup (180 g) dried black beans, rinsed
3 cups (700 ml) water

1 Add the black beans and water to the pressure cooking pot and stir. Lock the lid in place. Select High Pressure and 30 minutes cook time.

2 When the cook time ends, turn off the pressure cooker. Let the pressure release naturally for 20 minutes, then finish with a quick pressure release. When the float valve drops, carefully remove the lid.

3 Remove the black beans from the pressure cooking pot and allow to cool for 20 minutes.

4 To serve, you can mash or use a food mill or blender to puree. (Add water if needed to blend but use the minimum amount necessary.)

Tips

If you're worried about the beans making your baby gassy, use the quick soak method. Place the rinsed black beans in the pressure cooking pot and add enough water to cover the beans by 2 inches (5 cm). Lock the lid in place. Select High Pressure and 1 minute cook time.

When the cook time ends, turn off the pressure cooker. Let the beans soak for 1 hour. Remove the lid. Discard any beans that are floating on top of the water, then strain the beans. Discard the cooking water and rinse out the pressure cooking pot.

Return the soaked beans to the pot with 1 cup (235 ml) water and cook at High Pressure for 6 to 8 minutes. Continue with the recipe as directed.

Chickpeas

Like other legumes, chickpeas are a great source of fiber and protein! If your baby has a sensitive tummy, introduce chickpeas a little at a time in combination with a vegetable or meat puree.

MAKES 2 CUPS (328 G).

1 cup (200 g) dried chickpeas, rinsed
3 cups (700 ml) water

1 Add the chickpeas and water to the pressure cooking pot and stir. Lock the lid in place. Select High Pressure and 40 minutes cook time.

2 When the cook time ends, turn off the pressure cooker. Let the pressure release naturally for 20 minutes, then finish with a quick pressure release. When the float valve drops, carefully remove the lid.

3 Remove the chickpeas from the cooking pot and allow to cool for 20 minutes.

4 To serve, you can mash or use a food mill or blender to puree. (Add water if needed to blend but use the minimum amount necessary.)

Tip

You can double the recipe and reserve a portion of the chickpea puree to make hummus for yourself.

Lentils

Lentils are a good source of protein, fiber, and iron. Mash them up to make a thickener for your meat and dinner purees.

MAKES 2 CUPS (396 G).

1 cup (192 g) dried green lentils
2 cups (475 ml) water

1 Spread the lentils on a shallow dish and check for any debris. Add the lentils to a fine-mesh strainer and rinse well.

2 Add the rinsed lentils and water to the pressure cooking pot and stir. Lock the lid in place. Select High Pressure and 15 minutes cook time.

3 When the cook time ends, turn off the pressure cooker. Let the pressure release naturally for 10 minutes, then finish with a quick pressure release. When the float valve drops, carefully remove the lid.

4 Remove the lentils from the pressure cooking pot and allow to cool for 20 minutes.

5 To serve, you can mash or use a food mill or blender to puree. (Add water if needed to blend but use the minimum amount necessary.)

Tip

Lentils come in a variety of colors. If your baby doesn't like the ones you serve, pick a different color and try again. Yellow, red, and orange lentils are generally quicker cooking than green or brown, so you may need to reduce the cook time.

Chapter 3

Fruit and Vegetable Blends

Once babies have shown that they can handle simple fruits, vegetables, and grains, you can expand into more robust flavor combinations. These combinations are meant to be blended with a little more texture, and they work well when mixed with grains, yogurt, or cottage cheese.

Recipes

Apple Banana Carrot Puree

Simple as A-B-C! Apples and carrots are a classic combination, and the banana lends an extra creaminess to the puree. We love this fruit-vegetable blend, and we think your baby will as well!

MAKES 2 CUPS (455 G).

3 large soft apples (such as Jonagold, Fuji, or Golden Delicious), peeled, cored, and quartered

3 carrots, peeled and cut into 2-inch (5 cm) pieces

1 medium fresh banana, peeled

1 Place a steamer basket in the bottom of the pressure cooking pot and add 1 cup (235 ml) water. Place the apple and carrot pieces inside the basket. Lock the lid in place. Select High Pressure and 4 minutes cook time.

2 When the cook time ends, turn off the pressure cooker. Let the pressure release naturally for 5 minutes, then finish with a quick pressure release. When the float valve drops, carefully remove the lid.

3 Remove the apples and carrots from the steamer basket, reserving the cooking water. Allow to cool for 20 minutes.

4 Transfer the cooked apples and carrots to a blender jar or food processer. Add the peeled banana and ¼ cup (60 ml) reserved cooking water. Blend until very smooth. (Add more water if needed to blend but use the minimum amount necessary.)

Tip

The riper the banana, the sweeter the puree will be. If you're worried about the puree being too sweet, add half the banana to the puree and dice the other half for finger food.

Blueberry Apple Spinach Puree

The sweet flavor of the apples and blueberries makes it easy for your baby to enjoy spinach.

MAKES ABOUT 2 CUPS (455 G).

3 large soft apples (such as Jonagold, Fuji, or Golden Delicious), peeled, cored, and quartered

1 cup (145 g) blueberries

1 cup (30 g) tightly packed fresh spinach

1 Place a steamer basket in the bottom of the pressure cooking pot and add 1 cup (235 ml) water. Place the apple pieces, blueberries, and spinach inside the basket. Lock the lid in place. Select High Pressure and 4 minutes cook time.

2 When the cook time ends, turn off the pressure cooker. Let the pressure release naturally for 5 minutes, then finish with a quick pressure release. When the float valve drops, carefully remove the lid.

3 Remove the apples, blueberries, and spinach from the steamer basket, reserving the cooking water. Allow to cool for 20 minutes.

4 Transfer the cooked apples, blueberries, and spinach to a blender jar or food processer. Add ½ cup (120 ml) reserved cooking water. Blend until very smooth. (Add more water if needed to blend but use the minimum amount necessary.)

Tip

This recipe is pretty flexible! If your baby tolerates the spinach well, try increasing the spinach to 2 cups (60 g). You may also want to add more blueberries to keep the blue color.

Banana Blueberry Pear Puree

This flavor combination is a fruit lover's dream! Our babies gobbled it up, and we've been known to steal a couple cubes of these frozen purees to make our own morning smoothies!

MAKES 2 CUPS (455 G).

3 large pears, peeled, cored, and quartered
1 cup (145 g) blueberries
1 medium fresh banana, peeled

1 Place a steamer basket in the bottom of the pressure cooking pot and add 1 cup (235 ml) water. Place the pear quarters and blueberries inside the steamer basket. Lock the lid in place. Select High Pressure and 4 minutes cook time.

2 When the cook time ends, turn off the pressure cooker and use a quick pressure release. When the float valve drops, carefully remove the lid.

3 Remove the pears and blueberries from the steamer basket, reserving the cooking water. Allow to cool for 20 minutes.

4 Transfer the cooked pears and blueberries to a blender jar or food processer. Add the peeled banana and ¼ cup (60 ml) reserved cooking water and blend until very smooth. (Add more cooking water if needed to blend but use the minimum amount necessary.)

Tip

You can use fresh or frozen blueberries in this puree without adjusting the cook time.

Mango Pear Zucchini Puree

This puree is an excellent introduction to mango, and mixing fruits and veggies provides your baby with the sweet taste they prefer and the added vitamins and minerals you know they need.

MAKES 3 CUPS (675 G).

2 pears, peeled, cored, and quartered
1 fresh zucchini, sliced into 2-inch (5 cm) pieces
2 cups (350 g) frozen mango chunks

1 Place a steamer basket in the bottom of the pressure cooking pot and add 1 cup (235 ml) water. Place the pears, zucchini, and mango inside the steamer basket. Lock the lid in place. Select High Pressure and 4 minutes cook time.

2 When the cook time ends, turn off the pressure cooker. Let the pressure release naturally for 5 minutes, then use a quick pressure release. When the float valve drops, carefully remove the lid.

3 Remove the pears, zucchini, and mango from the steamer basket, reserving the cooking water. Allow to cool for 20 minutes.

4 Transfer the cooked pears, zucchini, and mango to a blender jar or food processer and blend until very smooth. (Add reserved cooking water if needed to blend but use the minimum amount necessary.)

Tip

If desired, you can use fresh mango in this puree, just add it after cooking the zucchini and pears. If you'd rather avoid mango, substitute frozen peaches.

Orange Carrot Peach Puree

This beautiful orange puree is a sweet blend that babies will love. It's an excellent way to introduce your baby to citrus—cooking the orange makes it gentler on baby's tummy.

MAKES 2 CUPS (396 G).

Makes 1½ cups (340 g).

1 large orange, peeled and halved

2 carrots, peeled and cut into 2-inch (5 cm) pieces

2 large peaches, peeled, pitted, and sliced

1 Place a steamer basket in the bottom of the pressure cooking pot and add 1 cup (235 ml) water. Place the orange, carrots, and peaches inside the steamer basket. Lock the lid in place. Select High Pressure and 4 minutes cook time.

2 When the cook time ends, turn off the pressure cooker. Let the steam release naturally for 5 minutes, then finish with a quick pressure release. When the float valve drops, carefully remove the lid. Remove the orange, carrots, and peaches from the steamer basket, reserving the cooking water. Allow to cool for 20 minutes.

3 Transfer the cooked orange, carrots, and peaches to a blender jar or food processer and blend until very smooth. (Add reserved cooking water if needed to blend but use the minimum amount necessary.)

Tip

For thick carrots, cut in half lengthwise, then slice into 2-inch (5 cm) pieces.

Pear and Pineapple Puree

This sweet puree is loaded with vitamin C and antioxidants, and it smells so good that you'll want to have a bowlful with your baby.

MAKES 2 CUPS (455 G).

3 large pears, peeled, cored, and quartered

½ fresh pineapple, cored and diced

1 cup (235 ml) water

1 Place the pear quarters, pineapple pieces, and water in the pressure cooking pot. Lock the lid in place. Select High Pressure and 4 minutes cook time.

2 When the cook time ends, turn off the pressure cooker. Let the pressure release naturally for 5 minutes, then use a quick pressure release. When the float valve drops, carefully remove the lid. Remove the pear and pineapple using a slotted spoon, reserving the cooking water. Allow to cool for 20 minutes.

3 Transfer the pear and pineapple to a blender jar or food processer and blend until very smooth. (Add reserved cooking water if needed to blend but use the minimum amount necessary.)

Tip

If you want, you can add the other half of the pineapple to the Mango Pear Zucchini Puree (page 70) for a tropical twist. Or just dice the remaining half of the pineapple, place it on skewers, and grill it to enjoy yourself.

Strawberry Peach Banana Puree

The strawberries and peaches give this puree a vibrant pink color and the banana adds a smooth texture.

MAKES 2 CUPS (396 G).

3 large peaches, peeled, pitted, and sliced

2 cups (290 g) strawberries, hulled

1 medium fresh banana, peeled

1 Place a steamer basket in the bottom of the pressure cooking pot and add 1 cup (235 ml) water. Place the peaches and strawberries inside the steamer basket. Lock the lid in place. Select High Pressure and 4 minutes cook time.

2 When the cook time ends, turn off the pressure cooker. Let the steam release naturally for 10 minutes, then use a quick pressure release. When the float valve drops, carefully remove the lid.

3 Remove the peaches and strawberries from the steamer basket, reserving the cooking water. Allow to cool for 20 minutes.

4 Transfer the cooked peaches and strawberries to a blender jar or food processer and add the banana. Blend until very smooth. (Add reserved cooking water if needed to blend but use the minimum amount necessary.)

Tip

If desired, you can simply cut the peaches in half with the skin on and remove the pit. The skin will easily come off after pressure cooking.

Strawberry Applesauce

This classic fruit blend is a kid favorite for a reason—it's sweet and delicious! Making it at home allows you to control the sugar content, and the pressure cooker makes it quicker than ever.

MAKES 3 TO 4 CUPS (675 TO 900 G).

5 large soft apples (such as Jonagold, Fuji, or Golden Delicious), peeled, cored, and quartered

2 cups (290 g) strawberries, washed and hulled

1 Place a steamer basket in the bottom of the pressure cooking pot and add 1 cup (235 ml) water. Place the apples and strawberries inside the steamer basket. Lock the lid in place. Select High Pressure and 4 minutes cook time.

2 When the cook time ends, turn off the pressure cooker. Let the pressure release naturally for 5 minutes, then use a quick pressure release. When the float valve drops, carefully remove the lid.

3 Remove the apples and strawberries from the steamer basket, reserving the cooking water. Allow to cool for 20 minutes.

4 Place the steamed apples and strawberries in a blender jar or food processer. Add ¼ cup (60 ml) reserved cooking water and blend until very smooth. (Add more water if needed to blend but use the minimum amount necessary.)

Tip

Using red apples will make the puree sweeter, and green apples will make the puree more tart. We generally use two or three different kinds of apples to balance the flavor between sweet and tart.

Butternut Squash and Sweet Corn Puree

Turn a slightly sweet butternut squash into a beautiful puree. This was always one of our babies' favorites.

MAKES 1½ CUPS (340 G).

2 cups (280 g) frozen diced butternut squash
1 cup (164 g) frozen sweet corn

1 Place a steamer basket in the bottom of the pressure cooking pot and add 1 cup (235 ml) water. Place the butternut squash and corn inside the steamer basket. Lock the lid in place. Select High Pressure and 4 minutes cook time.

2 When the cook time ends, turn off the pressure cooker and use a quick pressure release. When the float valve drops, carefully remove the lid.

3 Remove the butternut squash and corn from the steamer basket, reserving the cooking water. Allow to cool for 20 minutes.

4 Transfer the cooked butternut squash and corn to a blender jar or food processer. Add ¼ cup (60 ml) reserved cooking water and blend until very smooth. (Add more water if needed to blend but use the minimum amount necessary.)

Tip

If using fresh butternut squash, follow the Butternut Squash recipe (page 41) to cook the squash, and steam the corn separately with a 0-minute cook time while the squash cools. See Peach Puree (page 38) for how to set your pressure cooker if it doesn't have a 0-minute cook time.

Carrot and Sweet Potato Puree

This classic flavor combination makes a bright orange puree that's loaded with potassium and vitamins A and C.

MAKES 3 CUPS (675 G).

4 fresh carrots, peeled and ends trimmed
1 large sweet potato, peeled and cut into 1-inch (1.3 cm) cubes

1 Place a steamer basket in the bottom of the pressure cooking pot and add 1 cup (235 ml) water. Place the carrots and sweet potato inside the steamer basket. Lock the lid in place. Select High Pressure and 8 minutes cook time.

2 When the cook time ends, turn off the pressure cooker. Let the pressure release naturally for 10 minutes, then finish with a quick pressure release. When the float valve drops, carefully remove the lid.

3 Remove the carrots and sweet potato from the steamer basket, reserving the cooking water. Allow to cool for 20 minutes.

4 Place the steamed carrots and sweet potato in a blender jar or food processer. Add ¾ cup (175 ml) reserved cooking water and blend until very smooth. (Add more water if needed to blend but use the minimum amount necessary.)

Tip

For recipes with longer cook times like this one, you can leave your carrots whole and they'll still cook through.

Green Bean and Sweet Corn Puree

If green beans are too bitter for your baby, try sweetening them with corn. This blend is a gorgeous light-green puree that just might change your baby's mind about beans.

MAKES 2 CUPS (455 G).

2 cups (248 g) frozen green beans
1 cup (164 g) frozen sweet corn

1 Place a steamer basket in the bottom of the pressure cooking pot and add 1 cup (235 ml) water. Place the green beans and corn inside the steamer basket. Lock the lid in place. Select High Pressure and 3 minutes cook time.

2 When the cook time ends, turn off the pressure cooker. Use a quick pressure release. When the float valve drops, carefully remove the lid.

Remove the green beans and corn from the steamer basket, reserving the cooking water. Allow to cool for 20 minutes.

3 Transfer the cooked green beans and corn to a blender jar or food processer. Add ½ cup (120 ml) reserved cooking water and blend until very smooth. (Add more water if needed to blend but use the minimum amount necessary.)

Tip

We used frozen green beans and frozen corn in this recipe because of the convenience and year-round great taste. However, if you wish to use fresh green beans and corn right off the cob, use 2 cups (200 g) fresh green beans, washed, trimmed, and diced into 2-inch (5 cm) pieces, and 1 ear fresh corn, shucked and broken in half. Cook at High Pressure for 3 minutes and use a quick pressure release.

Mashed Potatoes with Cauliflower

Cauliflower is a good source of vitamins and fiber, and it is a great way to get some nutrition into your mashed potatoes.

MAKES 2 CUPS (455 G).

2 medium-size russet potatoes, peeled and quartered
½ cup (50 g) chopped cauliflower florets

1 Place a steamer basket in the bottom of the pressure cooking pot and add 1 cup (235 ml) water. Place the potatoes and cauliflower inside the steamer basket. Lock the lid in place. Select High Pressure and 5 minutes cook time.

2 When the cook time ends, turn off the pressure cooker. Use a quick pressure release. When the float valve drops, carefully remove the lid. Use a fork to test the potatoes. If needed, relock the lid and cook at High Pressure for a few minutes more.

3 Remove the potatoes and cauliflower from the steamer basket, reserving the cooking water. Allow to cool for 20 minutes.

4 Use a ricer or baby food mill to mash the potatoes and cauliflower together until mostly smooth. Stir in ¼ cup (60 ml) reserved cooking water, a little at a time, until the potatoes are the desired texture.

Tip

Reserve some of the mashed potatoes and cauliflower puree. Add milk, butter, salt, and pepper to taste and you've made a delicious and healthy side dish for your meal. Make a double or triple batch to feed your whole family.

Sweet Corn, Spaghetti Squash, and Spinach Puree

This vegetable blend is a baby favorite—the sweetness of the corn and spaghetti squash soften the sharp taste of spinach.

MAKES 3 CUPS (675 G).

1 fresh spaghetti squash (about 2 pounds, or 900 g)
1 cup (164 g) frozen corn
1 cup (30 g) tightly packed fresh spinach

1 Wash the spaghetti squash. Do not peel. Use a sharp knife to remove the stem end of the squash, then cut the squash in half vertically and remove the seeds with a spoon.

2 Place a trivet in the bottom of the pressure cooking pot and add 1 cup (235 ml) water. Carefully place the spaghetti squash pieces on top. Lock the lid in place. Select High Pressure and 8 minutes cook time.

3 When the cook time ends, turn off the pressure cooker. Let the pressure release naturally for 2 minutes, then finish with a quick pressure release. When the float valve drops, carefully remove the lid.

4 Remove the spaghetti squash from the pressure cooking pot, reserving the cooking water. Allow to cool until comfortable to handle, then remove the skin. Divide the spaghetti squash in half. Use one half for this recipe and set aside the other half.

5 Place a steamer basket in the bottom of the pressure cooking pot and add 1 cup (235 ml) water. Place the corn and spinach inside the steamer basket. Lock the lid in place. Select High Pressure and 0 minutes cook time.

6 When the cook time ends, turn off the pressure cooker. Use a quick pressure release. When the float valve drops, carefully remove the lid.

7 Remove the corn and spinach from the steamer basket. Discard the cooking water. Allow to cool for 20 minutes.

8 Place the cooked spaghetti squash, corn, and spinach in a blender jar or food processer. Add ½ cup (120 ml) reserved squash cooking water and blend until very smooth. (Add more water if needed to blend but use the minimum amount necessary.)

Tip

This recipe is easily doubled with no change to the cook time if you'd like to use the entire spaghetti squash. Or substitute the other half of the spaghetti squash for the frozen butternut squash in the Butternut Squash and Sweet Corn Puree (page 76).

Sweet Pea, Zucchini, and Green Bean Puree

Get your greens! The sweet peas and mild zucchini balance the green bean flavor in this all-vegetable blend.

MAKES 2 CUPS (455 G).

2 cups shelled peas, (300 g) fresh or (260 g) frozen

1 fresh zucchini, sliced into 2-inch (5 cm) pieces

1 cup (124 g) frozen green beans

1 Place a steamer basket in the bottom of the pressure cooking pot and add 1 cup (235 ml) water. Place the peas, zucchini, and green beans inside the basket. Lock the lid in place. Select High Pressure and 3 minutes cook time.

2 When the cook time ends, turn off the pressure cooker. Use a quick pressure release. When the float valve drops, carefully remove the lid.

3 Remove the vegetables from the steamer basket, reserving the cooking water. Allow to cool for 20 minutes.

4 Place the steamed vegetables in a blender jar or food processer. Add ¼ cup (60 ml) reserved cooking water and blend until very smooth. (Add more water if needed to blend but use the minimum amount necessary.)

Tip

If substituting fresh green beans, add 2 minutes to the cook time.

Sweet Pea and Avocado Puree

Avocados are a fantastic food for babies; they're high in potassium and fiber, and they give this pea puree a smooth and creamy texture.

MAKES 2 CUPS (455 G).

2 cups shelled peas; (300 g) fresh or (260 g) frozen

1 large avocado, halved, pitted, and peeled

1 Place a steamer basket in the bottom of the pressure cooking pot and add 1 cup (235 ml) water. Place the peas inside the steamer basket. Lock the lid in place. Select High Pressure and 2 minutes cook time.

2 When the cook time ends, turn off the pressure cooker. Use a quick pressure release. When the float valve drops, carefully remove the lid.

Remove the peas from the steamer basket, reserving the cooking water. Allow to cool for 20 minutes.

3 Transfer the cooked peas to a blender jar or food processer. Add the avocado and 1 cup (235 ml) reserved cooking water. Blend until very smooth. (Add more water if needed to blend but use the minimum amount necessary.)

Tip

Avocados are loaded with healthy fats and are a wonderful addition to baby's diet. Our testers didn't have any problem with them browning in this recipe; however, if you're worried, you can add a little mashed avocado to individual servings of pea puree.

Chapter 4

Meats and Dinners for Babies

Our babies didn't enjoy the store-bought baby food meats; however, they loved when we started serving them homemade dishes that included meat. This section begins with single-ingredient meats and then expands to include simple meat and veggie dinners. If your baby is hesitant to accept meats at first, try serving them with a favorite vegetable puree.

Recipes

Chicken Puree

Chicken is high in protein and B vitamins, and it makes an ideal first meat for baby. This simple chicken puree calls for chicken thighs, which have a higher fat content and cook up moist and tender in the pressure cooker.

MAKES 2 CUPS (455 G).

1 pound (455 g) boneless skinless chicken thighs, trimmed and diced
1 fresh carrot, peeled and cut into 2-inch (5 cm) pieces, optional, for color
1 cup (235 ml) water

1 Add the chicken, carrot (if using), and water to the pressure cooking pot. Lock the lid in place. Select High Pressure and 4 minutes cook time.

2 When the cook time ends, turn off the pressure cooker. Use a quick pressure release. When the float valve drops, carefully remove the lid.

3 Use an instant-read thermometer to check the chicken for doneness (see page 25). Remove the chicken and carrot from the cooking pot, reserving the cooking water. (You can skim off the fat if you prefer.) Allow to cool until comfortable to handle.

4 Place the chicken in a blender jar or food processer. Pulse the blender to grind the meat, adding a little reserved cooking water if necessary to blend. If you're using a high-powered blender to blend the chicken completely smooth, you'll need less water than if you want it to remain textured. Add ½ to ¾ cup (120 to 175 ml) reserved cooking water and blend until the desired consistency is reached. (Add more water if needed to blend but use the minimum amount necessary.)

Tip

If you prefer, you can use diced chicken breasts without changing the cook time.

Turkey Puree

Turkey contains more protein, B vitamins, and iron than chicken and is lower in cholesterol. It's another great first meat for baby.

MAKES 2 CUPS (455 G).

1 pound (455 g) fresh ground turkey
1 fresh carrot, peeled and cut into 2-inch (5 cm) pieces, optional, for color

1 Place a trivet in the bottom of the pressure cooking pot and add 1 cup (235 ml) water. Carefully place the ground turkey on top (no need to break up the ground turkey) followed by the carrot (if using). Lock the lid in place. Select High Pressure and 6 minutes cook time.

2 When the cook time ends, turn off the pressure cooker. Let the pressure release naturally for 2 minutes, then finish with a quick pressure release. When the float valve drops, carefully remove the lid.

3 Use an instant-read thermometer to check the cooked ground turkey for doneness (see page 25). Remove the ground turkey from the cooking pot, reserving the cooking water. (You can skim off the fat if you prefer.) Allow to cool until comfortable to handle.

4 Place the ground turkey in a blender jar or food processer. Pulse the blender to grind the meat, adding a little reserved cooking water if necessary to blend. If you're using a high-powered blender to blend the turkey completely smooth, you'll need less water than if you want it to remain textured. Add ½ to 1 cup (120 to 235 ml) reserved cooking water and blend until the desired consistency is reached. (Add more water if needed to blend but use the minimum amount necessary.)

Tips

Check your ground turkey to be sure no additional ingredients or spices have been added. This cook time is for fresh, not frozen, turkey that is in a flat block from the grocery store. If your ground turkey is in a round tube shape, you will need more time at high pressure. You can also use this method and cook time to cook ground chicken or ground beef for your baby.

If you prefer, you can also use 1 pound (455 g) of diced turkey in this recipe. Just place the diced turkey directly in the 1 cup (235 ml) water on the bottom of the pressure cooking pot and cook as directed.

Pork Puree

While cured meats like ham are best avoided with babies, lean cuts of pork are high in protein and B vitamins and low in fat. This simple puree is an excellent way to introduce your baby to pork.

MAKES 1½ TO 2 CUPS (340 TO 455 G).

1 pound (455 g) boneless center-cut pork chops, diced
1 to 2 tablespoons (16 g to 32 g) tomato paste, optional, for color
1 cup (235 ml) water

1 Add the pork, tomato paste (if using), and water to the pressure cooking pot. Lock the lid in place. Select High Pressure and 15 minutes cook time.

2 When the cook time ends, turn off the pressure cooker. Let the pressure release naturally for 10 minutes, then use a quick pressure release. When the float valve drops, carefully remove the lid.

3 Use an instant-read thermometer to check the pork for doneness (see page 25). Remove the cooked pork from the cooking pot, reserving the cooking water. Allow to cool until comfortable to handle.

4 Place the cooked pork in a blender jar or food processer. Pulse the blender to grind the meat, adding a little reserved cooking water if necessary to blend. If you're using a high-powered blender to blend the pork completely smooth, you'll need less water than if you want it to remain textured. Add ½ to ¾ cup (120 to 175 ml) reserved cooking water and blend until the desired consistency is reached. (Add more water if needed to blend but use the minimum amount necessary.)

Tip

For older babies, make a chunky puree and serve over the Mashed Potatoes with Cauliflower (page 79).

Beef Puree

Beef is a good source of iron, which is particularly important for breastfed babies.

MAKES 1½ TO 2 CUPS (340 TO 455 G).

1 pound (455 g) beef stew meat, diced (We use cross-rib roast)

1 to 2 tablespoons (16 g to 32 g) tomato paste, optional, for color

1 cup (235 ml) water

1 Add the beef, tomato paste (if using) and water to the pressure cooking pot. Lock the lid in place. Select High Pressure and 18 minutes cook time.

2 When the cook time ends, turn off the pressure cooker. Let the pressure release naturally for 5 minutes, then use a quick pressure release. When the float valve drops, carefully remove the lid.

3 Use an instant-read thermometer to check the beef for doneness (see page 25). Remove the cooked beef from the cooking pot, reserving the cooking water. Allow to cool until comfortable to handle.

4 Place the cooked beef in a blender jar or food processer. Pulse the blender to grind the meat, adding a little reserved cooking water if necessary to blend. If you're using a high-powered blender to blend the beef completely smooth, you'll need less water than if you want it to remain textured. Add ¼ to ½ cup (60 to 120 ml) reserved cooking water and blend until the desired consistency is reached. (Add more water if needed to blend but use the minimum amount necessary.)

Tip

If you're serving this as a first food and your baby hasn't yet been introduced to tomatoes, omit the tomato paste. However, the tomato paste adds a great color to the meat and makes it look much more appetizing for baby. Be sure to read the ingredients list and select a tomato paste that doesn't include salt or extra seasonings.

Beef Stew with Carrot, Celery, and Potato

For older babies, this beef stew tastes even better if you brown the beef in a little olive oil before you cook it at high pressure.

MAKES 2 CUPS (455 G).

1 pound (455 g) beef stew meat, diced (we use cross-rib roast)
1 tablespoon (16 g) tomato paste, (optional) for color
1 cup (235 ml) water or low-sodium beef broth
3 fresh carrots, peeled and finely diced
1 rib celery, finely diced
1 small russet potato, peeled and finely diced

1 Add the diced beef, tomato paste (if using), and water or low-sodium beef broth to the pressure cooking pot. Lock the lid in place. Select High Pressure and 17 minutes cook time.

2 When the cook time ends, turn off the pressure cooker and use a quick pressure release. When the float valve drops, carefully remove the lid. Add the vegetables to a steamer basket and place it in the pressure cooker above the beef. Lock the lid in place and select High Pressure and 1 minute cook time.

3 When the cook time ends, turn off the pressure cooker. Allow the pressure to release naturally for 5 minutes, then use a quick pressure release. Remove the steamer basket and vegetables from the cooking pot. Set aside.

4 Use an instant-read thermometer to check the beef for doneness (see page 25). Use a slotted spoon to remove the beef from the pressure cooker, reserving the cooking water. Allow to cool until comfortable to handle.

5 Place about three-quarters of the beef in a blender jar or food processer. Add 1 cup (235 ml) reserved cooking water or low-sodium beef broth and blend until the desired consistency is reached. (Add more water if needed to blend but use the minimum amount necessary.) Add the remaining portion of beef and pulse to dice the beef without pureeing it.

6 Mix in the steamed vegetables with a spoon. If desired, pulse the vegetables in the blender or food processor to the desired consistency.

Tip

Dice the carrots, celery, and potatoes into ½ pieces to avoid choking hazards. Before serving, make sure the beef you serve your baby is well diced and each bite is separated into individual pieces.

Chicken and Rice

This mix of chicken and rice can be as smooth or as textured as you like. Add diced vegetables and it's a complete meal!

MAKES 1½ TO 2 CUPS (340 TO 455 G).

1 pound (455 g) (about 4) boneless skinless chicken thighs, trimmed, diced
1 fresh carrot, peeled and cut into 2-inch (5 cm) pieces
1⅔ cup (395 ml) water or low-sodium chicken broth, divided
½ cup (98 g) white rice
½ cup (91 g) frozen diced vegetable mix, steamed, optional

1 Add diced chicken, carrot, and 1 cup (235 ml) water or low-sodium chicken broth to the pressure cooking pot. Place a trivet above the items in the cooking pot.

2 In a 7-inch (18 cm) cake pan, stir together the rice and ⅔ cup (160 ml) water. Use a sling to lower the pan carefully onto the trivet. Lock the lid in place. Select High Pressure and 4 minutes cook time.

3 When the cook time ends, turn off the pressure cooker. Let the pressure release naturally for 7 minutes, then finish with a quick pressure release. When the float valve drops, carefully remove the lid. Use the sling to remove the pan from the pressure cooking pot. Stir the rice well and allow to cool.

4 Use an instant-read thermometer to check the chicken for doneness (see page 25). Remove the diced chicken and carrot from the cooking pot, reserving the cooking water. Allow to cool until comfortable to handle.

5 Place the diced chicken and carrot in a blender jar or food processor. Add ¾ cup (175 ml) reserved cooking water and blend until the desired consistency is reached. (Add more water if needed to blend but use the minimum amount necessary.)

6 If using, pulse the steamed vegetables in the blender or food processor to the desired consistency. Add as much rice as desired and mix with a spoon.

Tip

Reserve some of the chicken for older eaters. Add it to the blender jar after pureeing and pulse two or three times to shred. Remove from the blender jar and add steamed rice and vegetables, if desired.

Turkey and Vegetable Medley

This classic combination features lean turkey and nutritious vegetables in a blend your baby will love.

MAKES 2 CUPS (455 G).

1 pound (455 g) turkey breast, diced
1 fresh carrot, peeled and cut into 2-inch (5 cm) pieces
1½ cups (355 ml) water or reduced-sodium chicken broth or turkey stock
½ cup (91 g) frozen diced vegetable mix, steamed

1 Add the diced turkey, carrot, and water to the pressure cooking pot. Lock the lid in place. Select High Pressure and 6 minutes cook time.

2 When the cook time ends, turn off the pressure cooker. Let the pressure release naturally for 2 minutes, then finish with a quick pressure release. When the float valve drops, carefully remove the lid.

3 Use an instant-read thermometer to check the turkey for doneness (see page 25). Remove the cooked turkey and carrot from the cooking pot, reserving the cooking water. Allow to cool until comfortable to handle.

4 For older eaters, reserve and shred some of the cooked turkey. Place the cooked turkey and carrot in a blender jar or food processer. Add 1½ cups (355 ml) reserved cooking water and blend until the desired consistency is reached. (Add more water if needed to blend but use the minimum amount necessary.)

5 Add the steamed vegetables and mix with a spoon. If desired, pulse the vegetables in the blender or food processor to the desired consistency.

Tip

Steam your frozen vegetables in the pressure cooker while the turkey cools. Place a steamer basket and 1 cup (235 ml) water in the pressure cooker pot. Add the frozen vegetables and select a 0-minute cook time. (See the tip on page 38 for how to set your pressure cooker if it doesn't have a 0-minute cook time.) Finish with a quick pressure release.

Chicken and Pasta in Butternut Squash Puree

The thick butternut squash puree makes this a wholesome meal for babies learning to use a spoon.

MAKES 2 CUPS (455 G).

½ pound (225 g) boneless skinless chicken thighs, diced into baby-size pieces (less than ½ inch [1.3 cm] in all directions)

¼ cup (42 g) orzo pasta

1 cup (235 ml) water or low-sodium chicken broth

3 cups (420 g) frozen diced butternut squash

1 Add the diced chicken, orzo, and water or low-sodium chicken broth to the pressure cooking pot. Place a steamer basket inside the cooking pot and place the butternut squash on top. Lock the lid in place. Select High Pressure and 4 minutes cook time.

2 When the cook time ends, turn off the pressure cooker. Let the pressure release naturally for 5 minutes, then finish with a quick pressure release. When the float valve drops, carefully remove the lid. Remove the steamer basket and butternut squash from the cooking pot. Set aside.

3 Use an instant-read thermometer to check the chicken for doneness (see page 25). Use a slotted spoon to remove the chicken and orzo from the pressure cooker, reserving the cooking water. Allow to cool until comfortable to handle.

4 Place the butternut squash in a blender jar or food processer. Add ¼ cup (60 ml) reserved cooking water and blend until the desired consistency is reached. (Add more water if needed to blend but use the minimum amount necessary.) Remove to a bowl and mix in the chicken and orzo with a spoon.

Tip

Orzo pastas can have a broad range of cook times. This recipe was written for orzo with a packaged stovetop cook time between 8 and 11 minutes. If you don't have orzo pasta on hand, you can substitute couscous with no change to the cook time.

Butternut Squash Dinner

Butternut squash and carrots blend together in a slightly sweet, orange base, and the couscous adds a fun texture for babies who are ready to move beyond purees.

MAKES 2 CUPS (455 G).

2 cups (280 g) frozen diced butternut squash
2 fresh carrots, peeled and cut into 2-inch (5 cm) pieces
1 ¾ cups (410 ml) water, divided
½ cup (86 g) pearl couscous

1 Add the squash, carrots, and 1 cup (235 ml) water to the bottom of the pressure cooking pot. Place a trivet above the items in the pressure cooking pot.

2 In a 7-inch (18 cm) cake pan, stir together the couscous and remaining ¾ cup (175 ml) water. Use a sling to lower the pan carefully onto the trivet. Lock the lid in place. Select High Pressure and 5 minutes cook time.

3 When the cook time ends, turn off the pressure cooker. Allow the pressure to release naturally for 2 minutes, then finish with a quick pressure release. When the float valve drops, carefully remove the lid. Use the sling to remove the pan from the pressure cooking pot. Stir the couscous well and allow to cool.

4 Place a fine-mesh strainer above a bowl to separate the squash and carrots from the cooking water, reserving the cooking water. Place the squash and carrots in a blender with ¼ cup (60 ml) reserved cooking water. Blend until smooth. Stir in as much couscous as desired.

Tip

Add tomatoes or corn to this dinner before pressure cooking for even more vegetable goodness.

Fresh Garden Vegetable and Pasta Medley

This pasta and vegetable meal is not in a puree to allow your baby to enjoy different colors and textures. Be sure to dice your vegetables finely—less than ½ inch (1.3 cm) in all directions—to make sure it's safe for baby.

MAKES 2 CUPS (455 G).

½ cup (84 g) orzo pasta

1 cup (235 ml) water

1 cup (130 g) peeled, diced carrots

1 cup (120 g) diced zucchini

1 cup (120 g) diced yellow squash

1 Add the orzo and water to the pressure cooking pot. Place a steamer basket on top and add the carrots, zucchini, and yellow squash to the steamer. Lock the lid in place. Select High Pressure and 3 minutes cook time.

2 When the cook time ends, turn off the pressure cooker. Let the pressure release naturally for 3 minutes, then finish with a quick pressure release. When the float valve drops, carefully remove the lid. Remove the steamer basket and vegetables from the cooking pot. Set aside. Use a slotted spoon to remove the orzo from the pressure cooker. Allow to cool until comfortable to handle.

3 Mix the orzo pasta with the vegetables.

Tip

You can substitute your baby's favorite vegetables, just make sure they are cut into baby-size pieces.

Chapter 5

Desserts for a First Birthday Celebration

Jennifer's babies didn't get foods with added sugar until their first birthday, and even then, she liked to keep the sugar content low. Barbara fed her babies healthy foods but allowed for the occasional indulgence. Therefore, for this chapter, we created one recipe in each style to help you celebrate this happy milestone: one healthier, no-sugar-added carrot cake and one finger-licking introduction to chocolate for these fun smash cakes.

Recipes

Healthy Carrot Smash Cake with Cream Cheese Frosting

The first birthday is such a happy milestone! Celebrate the big day with this no-sugar-added carrot cake that's lightly sweetened with just maple syrup.

MAKES ONE 4-INCH (10 CM) SMASH CAKE.

Nonstick baking spray with flour

⅓ cup (42 g) all-purpose flour

½ teaspoon baking powder

¾ teaspoon pumpkin pie spice

⅛ teaspoon salt

3 tablespoons (45 ml) maple syrup

2 tablespoons olive oil

2 tablespoons milk

1 egg yolk

½ teaspoon vanilla extract

¼ cup finely grated carrot

¼ cup (35 g) raisins

CREAM CHEESE FROSTING

2 tablespoons (30 ml) cream cheese, softened

2 tablespoons (30 ml) plain Greek yogurt

1 tablespoon (15 ml) pure maple syrup

Tip

To make your own pumpkin pie spice, mix ½ teaspoon ground cinnamon, ¼ teaspoon ground ginger, ¼ teaspoon ground nutmeg, and ⅛ teaspoon ground cloves for 1 teaspoon pumpkin pie spice.

1 Coat a 4-inch (10 cm) cake pan with nonstick baking spray with flour.

2 In a small bowl, add the flour, baking powder, pumpkin pie spice, and salt, and whisk until combined. Set aside.

3 In a large mixing bowl, whisk the maple syrup, olive oil, milk, egg yolk, and vanilla together until well-blended. Add the dry ingredients and mix until just blended. Fold in the carrots and raisins. Spoon the batter into the prepared pan.

4 Pour 1 cup (235 ml) water into the pressure cooker cooking pot and place a trivet in the bottom. Carefully center the filled pan on a sling and lower the pan onto the trivet. Lock the lid in place. Select High Pressure and 16 minutes cook time.

5 When the cook time ends, turn off the pressure cooker. Let the pressure release naturally for 10 minutes, then finish with a quick pressure release. When the float valve drops, carefully remove the lid.

6 With the sling, transfer the pan to a wire rack to cool, uncovered, for 5 minutes. Gently loosen the edges, remove the cake from the pan, transfer to a wire rack, and cool completely.

7 *Prepare the cream cheese frosting:* In a large bowl, combine the cream cheese, yogurt, and maple syrup. Using a handheld electric mixer, mix the ingredients on medium speed until smooth. Spread on top of the cooled cake and decorate as desired.

Chocolate–Chocolate Smash Cake

There's nothing quite like baby's first taste of chocolate cake! This cute little smash cake is topped with a rich, easy-to-make chocolate ganache that your one-year-old will be licking off their sweet little fingers.

MAKES ONE 4-INCH (10 CM) SMASH CAKE.

Nonstick baking spray with flour

3 tablespoons (45 ml) milk

2 tablespoons (28 ml) olive oil

1 large egg yolk

1 teaspoon vanilla extract

¼ cup (50 g) sugar

¼ cup (31 g) all-purpose flour

2 tablespoons (10 g) cocoa powder

½ teaspoon baking powder

⅛ teaspoon salt

CHOCOLATE GANACHE

1 tablespoon (15 ml) heavy cream

1½ ounces (42 g) milk chocolate, finely chopped

Sprinkles or chocolate curls for decorating

1 Coat a 4-inch (10 cm) cake pan with nonstick baking spray with flour.

2 In a large bowl, whisk the milk, oil, egg yolk, and vanilla until blended. Whisk in the sugar. Put a fine-mesh strainer over the top of the bowl and add the flour, cocoa powder, baking powder, and salt. Shake to sift the ingredients into the mixing bowl with the wet ingredients, and whisk just until blended. Pour into the prepared pan.

3 Pour 1 cup (235 ml) water into the pressure cooking pot and place a trivet in the bottom. Carefully center the filled pan on a sling and lower the pan onto the trivet. Lock the lid in place. Select High Pressure and 13 minutes cook time.

4 When the cook time ends, turn off the pressure cooker. Let the pressure release naturally for 10 minutes, then finish with a quick pressure release. When the float valve drops, carefully remove the lid. Transfer the pan to a wire rack to cool for 5 minutes. Run a knife around the edge to loosen the cake, then invert onto the rack to cool completely.

5 *Prepare the chocolate ganache*: In a small microwave-safe dish, heat the cream in the microwave just until it starts to bubble around the edges. Add the chopped chocolate and stir until smooth. (If necessary, heat in the microwave on medium power to melt the chocolate.) Allow the ganache to cool on the counter until it is thick and spreadable. Spoon the ganache on top of the cooled cake. Decorate with sprinkles or chocolate curls as desired.

Tip

Using olive oil cuts saturated fat in your baking and adds antioxidants and vitamin E to your baked goods. The olive oil in this recipe doesn't add a strong flavor, but it has natural emulsifiers that help keep the cake moist and delicious. If you prefer, you can substitute vegetable oil.

Part

two

Toddler Food

Chapter 6

Breakfasts for Toddlers

Start the day off with a variety of sweet and savory meals that both you and your toddler will love. Many of these recipes can be made ahead and warmed up in the morning when you and your toddler are ready to start the day.

Recipes

Evan's Lemon Berry Breakfast Risotto

Jennifer's son is proud to have helped create this recipe—he listed the ingredients he'd like (all his favorite flavors)—and we love how it turned out. He likes to go heavy on the berries, so we generally dice double the berries called for here.

MAKES 4 SERVINGS.

2 tablespoons (28 g) unsalted butter

1½ cups (270 g) Arborio rice

4 cups (945 ml) unsweetened almond milk, plus more for serving

2 to 4 tablespoons (26 to 50 g) sugar

Zest of 1 lemon

1 tablespoon (15 ml) lemon juice

1 teaspoon vanilla extract, optional

¼ teaspoon salt

1½ cups diced (255 g) strawberries, (190 g) raspberries, (220 g) blackberries, or (220 g) blueberries, for serving

Tip

We love the flavor and texture that almond milk gives this dish; however, if you wish, you can substitute 1 cup (235 ml) heavy cream or half-and-half and 3 cups (700 ml) water for the almond milk. Don't substitute milk in a 1:1 ratio because the lemon juice can cause the milk to curdle slightly while cooking.

1 Select Sauté and melt the butter in the pressure cooking pot. Stir in the rice and cook for 3 to 4 minutes, stirring frequently, until the rice becomes opaque. Stir in the almond milk, sugar, lemon zest, lemon juice, vanilla, and salt. Lock the lid in place. Select High Pressure and 6 minutes cook time.

2 When the cook time ends, turn off the pressure cooker. Let the pressure release naturally for 5 minutes, then finish with a quick pressure release. When the float valve drops, carefully remove the lid.

3 Remove the pressure cooking pot from the housing. Stir the risotto to mix in any liquid that may have settled on the top. (The mixture will continue to thicken as it cools; however, if there's more liquid than you like, select Sauté and cook to the desired consistency.)

4 Serve topped with diced fresh berries and a splash of almond milk.

Banana Cream Breakfast Risotto

Most kids love bananas, and your family will go bananas for this smooth, creamy breakfast risotto. It's a fun way to start the day!

MAKES 4 SERVINGS.

2 tablespoons (28 g) unsalted butter

1½ cups (270 g) Arborio rice

3 cups (700 ml) water

1 cup (235 ml) heavy cream, plus more for serving

1 tablespoon (14 g) brown sugar, plus more for serving

1 teaspoon vanilla extract

¼ teaspoon salt

2 to 4 ounces (55 to 115 g) cream cheese, at room temperature, cubed

1 fresh banana, well mashed

1 to 2 fresh bananas, thinly sliced

Whipped cream for serving, optional

Tip

If you're dishing up individual servings each day, only slice as much fresh banana as you need and add the fresh banana after reheating. To reheat, stir in additional cream, milk, or water, and microwave on 50 percent power until the risotto reaches the desired temperature.

1 Select Sauté and melt the butter in the pressure cooking pot. Stir in the rice and cook for 3 to 4 minutes, stirring frequently, until the rice becomes opaque. Stir in the water, heavy cream, brown sugar, vanilla, and salt. Lock the lid in place. Select High Pressure and 6 minutes cook time.

2 When the cook time ends, turn off the pressure cooker. Let the pressure release naturally for 5 minutes, then finish with a quick pressure release. When the float valve drops, carefully remove the lid.

3 Remove the pressure cooking pot from the housing. Stir the risotto to mix in any liquid that may have settled on the top. (The mixture will continue to thicken as it cools.) Stir in the cream cheese and mashed banana.

4 Serve topped with fresh banana slices, a sprinkle of brown sugar (if desired), and a splash of cream or a dollop of whipped cream, if desired.

Fruit Cocktail Steel Cut Oats

Colorful fruit cocktail is generally less expensive than fresh fruit and is available year-round. Feel better about serving this kid favorite by using it as a topping for some hearty, long-lasting oats.

MAKES 4 SERVINGS.

1 tablespoon (14 g) unsalted butter

1 cup (80 g) steel cut oats

2 ¼ cups (550 ml) water

½ cup (120 ml) heavy cream

1 teaspoon vanilla extract

⅛ teaspoon salt

1 can (15 ounces [425 g]) or
4 containers (4 ounces [115 g] each)
fruit cocktail in water or 100% juice

1 Select Sauté and melt the butter in the pressure cooking pot. Add the oats. Toast for about 3 minutes, stirring constantly, until they smell nutty. Stir in the water, heavy cream, vanilla, and salt. Lock the lid in place. Select High Pressure and 10 minutes cook time.

2 While the oats cook, strain the fruit cocktail over a cup, reserving the juice.

3 When the cook time ends, turn off the pressure cooking pot. Let the pressure release naturally for 10 minutes, then finish with a quick pressure release. When the float valve drops, carefully remove the lid. Stir the cooked oats in the pressure cooking pot. (They will be quite thick.) Add the drained fruit and enough reserved juice to bring the oats to the desired consistency. Stir to combine. These oats get thicker as they cool; if the consistency becomes thicker than desired, stir in additional reserved fruit juice, heavy cream, or water as needed.

Tip

If you're dishing up individual servings each day, one 4-ounce (115 g) container of fruit cocktail is about the right amount for 1 serving of steel cut oats. You may still want to reserve some of the juice because thicker oats will be easier for toddlers to eat. To reheat, stir in additional reserved fruit juice, cream, or water and microwave on 50 percent power until the oats reach the desired temperature.

Tip

Chia seeds are an excellent thickener and an easy way to add omega-3 fatty acids to your toddler's diet. If your toddler is skeptical of the "black dots" in their food, use a coffee grinder or spice mill to grind the chia seeds prior to adding them to the oats. If you omit them, be sure to reduce the liquids added.

Pumpkin-Cranberry-Apple Steel Cut Oats

This delicious breakfast is the perfect blend of fall flavors. While the oats are a fun orange color and can stand alone, the cinnamon-pecan topping for adults and older children really takes this breakfast to the next level.

MAKES 4 SERVINGS.

1 cup (80 g) steel cut oats

2½ cups (590 ml) water

½ cup (120 ml) heavy cream

1 cup (245 g) pumpkin puree

¼ cup (60 ml) maple syrup, plus more for serving

2 teaspoons ground cinnamon

1 teaspoon pumpkin pie spice

¼ cup (30 g) dried cranberries

¼ teaspoon salt

1 or 2 fresh apples, peeled, cored, and diced

2 tablespoons (26 g) chia seeds

Milk, for serving

OPTIONAL CINNAMON-PECAN TOPPING

1 cup (225 g) packed brown sugar

¼ cup (60 ml) water

1 tablespoon (7 g) ground cinnamon

⅛ teaspoon salt

2 cups (220 g) roughly chopped pecans

1 Select Sauté and melt the butter in the pressure cooking pot. Add the oats. Toast for about 3 minutes, stirring constantly, until the oats smell nutty. Stir in the water, heavy cream, pumpkin puree, maple syrup, cinnamon, pumpkin pie spice, cranberries, and salt. Lock the lid in place. Select High Pressure and 10 minutes cook time.

2 When the cook time ends, turn off the pressure cooker. Let the pressure release naturally for 10 minutes, then finish with a quick pressure release. When the float valve drops, carefully remove the lid.

3 Stir the cooked oats in the pressure cooking pot. Add the diced apple and chia seeds and stir to combine. Replace the lid and let sit, covered, for 5 minutes.

4 *Prepare the topping:* While the oats are cooking, combine the brown sugar, water, cinnamon, and salt in a sauté pan. Bring to a boil over medium heat. (If your stove runs hot, cook over medium-low.) Add the pecans and cook, stirring constantly, until the liquid evaporates and leaves a candy coating on the pecan pieces. You can remove the pecans at any stage of this process: when the melted sugar becomes solid and sticks to the pecans and they become "sandy," which results in a more tender nut, or continue stirring until the sugar melts again and gives the pecans a shiny coating, which gives you more of a crunch. (We prefer stopping at the sandy stage when serving with the oats.) Watch closely to make sure they do not burn—especially if you're letting them go to the shiny stage.

5 Pour the pecans onto a baking sheet lined with parchment. Spread into a thin layer, separating the pecans as necessary. Let cool completely. (These can be made ahead of time, if desired.)

6 Serve topped with a splash of milk, a swirl of maple syrup, and the cinnamon-pecan topping (if using).

Rainbow Fruit Yogurt Parfaits

A colorful, delicious start to the day! This easy recipe allows you to make four different fruit compotes at the same time—and you can blend them and store them in the same jars they cook in!

MAKES 4 SERVINGS.

RED RASPBERRY-STRAWBERRY COMPOTE

½ cup raspberries, (65 g) fresh or (70 g) frozen

½ cup strawberries, (73 g) fresh or (75 g) frozen

1 tablespoon (15 ml) apple juice

YELLOW PEACH COMPOTE

1 cup (154 g) diced yellow peaches, (154 g) fresh or (140 g) frozen

1 tablespoon (15 ml) apple juice

GREEN PINEAPPLE COMPOTE

1 cup (165 g) chopped fresh pineapple

¾ cup (23 g) baby spinach leaves

1 tablespoon (15 ml) apple juice

BLUEBERRY COMPOTE

½ cup blueberries, (75 g) fresh or (78 g) frozen

½ cup blackberries, (75 g) fresh or (75 g) frozen

1 tablespoon (15 ml) apple juice

2 tablespoons (16 g) cornstarch, optional

2 tablespoons (28 ml) cold water, optional

1 pint (473 g) Greek store-bought or homemade yogurt, plain or vanilla flavor

Additional fresh fruit, for serving, optional

1 *Prepare the compotes:* In four separate wide-mouth pint-size (473 ml) mason jars, prepare the raspberry-strawberry, peach, pineapple, and blueberry compotes by combining the ingredients in each jar. Do not place lids on the mason jars.

2 Place a trivet in the bottom of the pressure cooking pot and add 1 cup (235 ml) water. Place the mason jars on top. Lock the lid in place. Select High Pressure and 2 minutes cook time.

3 When the cook time ends, turn off the pressure cooker. Let the pressure release naturally for 10 minutes. then finish with a quick pressure release. When the float valve drops, carefully remove the lid.

4 Remove the mason jars from the pressure cooking pot. Use an immersion blender directly in the mason jar to blend the compotes to the desired consistency. The compotes will thicken as they cool.

continued

5 If you'd like a thicker compote, in a small bowl, stir together cornstarch and 2 tablespoons (28 ml) cold water until well combined. Divide the slurry evenly among the four jars. Return the mason jars to the pressure cooker and select High Pressure and 0 minutes cook time. Remove mason jars and cool to room temperature, then refrigerate until ready to serve.

6 To serve rainbow style, in a cup, layer a spoonful of yogurt and a spoonful of the blueberry compote, then yogurt, and repeat with the green, yellow, and red compotes. Top with additional diced fresh fruit, if desired. (Or mix each color of compote with yogurt and serve in a compartmentalized serving dish.)

Tip

The wide-mouth pint-size (473 ml) mason jars come in two different shapes—wide and tall. You'll need the tall ones if you want to fit all four jars in a 6-quart (5.7 L) pressure cooker. You can find these jars in most big-box stores, some grocery stores, or online.

Blueberries and Cream Baked French Toast

Serving fun, indulgent breakfasts on the weekends is a tradition your kids are sure to remember. This French toast might just become a weekend breakfast staple in your house—the rich lemon cream is easy to make and is a great alternative to maple syrup.

MAKES 4 SERVINGS.

LEMON CREAM

4 ounces (115 g) cream cheese, at room temperature

2 tablespoons (40 g) lemon curd

1 tablespoon (13 g) sugar

½ cup (120 ml) heavy cream

½ teaspoon vanilla extract

BLUEBERRY FRENCH TOAST

Nonstick baking spray with flour

4 tablespoons (55 g) butter, melted

¼ cup (50 g) sugar

2 cups (475 ml) whole milk

3 eggs, beaten

1 teaspoon vanilla extract

¼ teaspoon salt

10 cups (500 g) cubed challah bread (about 1 loaf)

½ cup (75 g) fresh blueberries

Tip

The type of bread you use makes a big difference in how your baked French toast turns out. If you can't find challah bread, you can substitute another rich bread like brioche, Hawaiian sweet bread, or croissants. Other types of bread won't absorb as much liquid when cooked, so if you use a different type of bread, you'll need to reduce your liquids accordingly.

1 *Prepare the lemon cream:* Using a handheld mixer, in a small bowl, beat the cream cheese, lemon curd, and 1 tablespoon (13 g) sugar until smooth. Add the heavy cream and vanilla and beat until soft peaks form. Refrigerate until ready to serve. (We prefer to make this the night before.)

2 *Prepare the French toast:* Generously coat a 7-inch (18 cm) cake pan with nonstick baking spray with flour. In a large bowl, whisk together the melted butter and ¼ cup (50 g) sugar. Add the milk, beaten eggs, vanilla, and salt. Mix in the cubed bread. Let rest until the bread absorbs the milk, stirring occasionally. Gently stir in the fresh blueberries. Gently press the bread mixture into the prepared pan.

3 Pour 1 cup (235 ml) water (235 ml) into the pressure cooking pot and place a trivet in the bottom. Carefully center the filled pan on a sling and lower the pan onto the trivet. Lock the lid in place. Select High Pressure and 25 minutes cook time.

4 When the cook time ends, turn off the pressure cooker. Let the pressure release naturally for 5 minutes, then finish with a quick pressure release. When the float valve drops, carefully remove the lid. Use the sling to transfer the pan to a wire rack.

5 If desired, put the dish under a preheated broiler to crisp the top. Cut into slices and serve topped with a dollop of the lemon cream.

Banana Bread Bites

These fun-to-eat banana bread bites are the perfect size for little hands. Banana bread is a moist, dense bread that is perfect for cooking in the pressure cooker.

MAKES 14 BITES.

Nonstick baking spray with flour

1½ cups (188 g) all-purpose flour

1 teaspoon baking powder

¼ teaspoon baking soda

¼ teaspoon salt

1 cup (225 g) mashed very ripe banana (about 3 small)

⅓ cup (75 g) brown sugar

¼ cup (60 g) sour cream

3 tablespoons (42 g) unsalted butter, melted

½ teaspoon vanilla extract

1 large egg, beaten

¼ cup (28 g) chopped toasted pecans, (30 g) walnuts, or (28 g) slivered almonds, optional

¼ cup (35 g) dried cranberries, optional

Tip

This banana bread recipe has been in the family for decades. It's a forgiving recipe; you can make substitutions based on what you have on hand: Greek yogurt for sour cream, margarine for butter, even increase or decrease the sugar content. Play around with it and see what works best for your family!

1 Spray two silicone baby food trays with nonstick baking spray with flour. In a small bowl, sift together the flour, baking powder, baking soda, and salt. Set aside.

2 In a large bowl, combine the mashed bananas, brown sugar, sour cream, butter, and vanilla. Add the egg and, using a handheld electric mixer, beat at medium speed until well blended.

3 Fold in the dry ingredients, then gently mix in the nuts and cranberries (if using). Stir until just blended. Evenly divide the batter among the muffin cups; do not fill more than two-thirds full. Place a paper towel on top of the silicone tray and cover with aluminum foil.

4 Pour 1 cup (235 ml) water into the pressure cooking pot and place a trivet in the bottom. Use a sling to lower the silicone trays into the pot, carefully stacking one tray on top of the other. Lock the lid in place. Select High Pressure and 25 minutes cook time.

5 When the cook time ends, turn off the pressure cooker. Let the pressure release naturally for 5 minutes, then finish with a quick pressure release. When the float valve drops, carefully remove the lid and use the sling to remove the trays. Place on a wire rack and remove the foil and paper towel. Allow to cool for 10 minutes, then turn the cups over and gently squeeze to remove the muffins from the trays.

Blueberry Muffin Bites

Did you know you can "bake" in the pressure cooker? These light and fluffy muffins start with a muffin mix, so they're perfect when you need something quick and easy to put together.

MAKES 7 BITES.

Nonstick baking spray with flour

1 box (7 ounces [200 g]) blueberry muffin mix, prepared according to package directions

¼ cup (36 g) fresh blueberries

1 Generously coat one silicone baby food tray with nonstick baking spray with flour. In a small bowl, prepare the blueberry muffin mix. Set aside.

2 Place half of the muffin batter in the silicone tray, then distribute half of the blueberries evenly among the cups. Repeat with the remaining batter and blueberries. Do not fill the cups more than half full.

3 Place a paper towel on top of the silicone tray and cover tightly with aluminum foil.

4 Pour 1 cup (235 ml) water into the pressure cooking pot and place a trivet in the bottom. Use a sling to lower the silicone tray carefully into the pot. Lock the lid in place. Select High Pressure and 12 minutes cook time.

5 When the cook time ends, turn off the pressure cooker. Let the pressure release naturally for 5 minutes, then finish with a quick pressure release. When the float valve drops, carefully remove the lid.

6 With the sling, transfer the silicone tray to a wire rack. Remove the foil and paper towel. Cool for 5 minutes, uncovered. Gently loosen the edges, remove the muffins from the silicone tray, and cool on a wire rack.

Tip

If you wish, you can use a 16.9-ounce (475 g) box of premium blueberry muffin mix with canned blueberries. Each silicone baby food tray will fit half of the batter (approximately 6 ounces [170 g] of mix each). If you wish to mix up the whole box at one time, you'll still have best results if you pressure cook each tray individually. Keep the second tray of prepared muffin batter in the refrigerator while you wait for the first to cook.

Ham and Cheese Egg Bites

This recipe is super versatile, so change up the ingredients to match your toddler's tastes. To sneak in some vitamins with their protein, add their favorite baby food vegetable puree. This recipe is easily halved without changing the cooking time.

MAKES 14 BITES.

Nonstick cooking spray

6 large eggs

¼ cup (60 ml) milk, half-and-half, or heavy cream

¼ teaspoon salt

⅛ teaspoon freshly ground black pepper

¼ cup (55 g) vegetable puree (broccoli, carrot, spinach), optional

½ cup (75 g) diced ham or (40 g) precooked bacon

⅓ cup (30 g) shredded cheddar cheese

1 Spray two silicone baby food trays with nonstick cooking spray. In a large bowl, whisk the eggs, milk, salt, pepper, and vegetable puree (if using), until just blended. Evenly divide the ham among silicone cups. Pour the egg mixture over the ham until each cup is about two-thirds full. Sprinkle the cheddar cheese over each.

2 Pour 1 cup (235 ml) water into the pressure cooking pot and place a trivet in the bottom. Use a sling to lower the silicone trays, carefully stacking one on top of the other. Lock the lid in place. Select High Pressure and 9 minutes cook time for softer eggs or 11 minutes cook time for harder eggs.

3 When the cook time ends, turn off the pressure cooker. Let the pressure release naturally for 5 minutes, then finish with a quick pressure release. When the float valve drops, carefully remove the lid and use the sling to remove the trays. Place on a wire rack to cool for 5 minutes, then turn the tray over and gently squeeze to remove the egg bites from the silicone trays.

4 Serve whole or sliced with mini croissants or toast, if desired.

Tip

You don't have to make all of the egg bites toddler-friendly! Make some for yourself by changing up the meats and cheeses or adding your own spices and mix-ins, such as:

- Green chilies and diced tomatoes

- Tomatoes, mozzarella cheese, and basil

- Bell peppers and matchstick carrots

- Finely sliced fresh spinach, diced sun-dried tomatoes, and Parmesan

No matter what fillings you add, make sure you fill the cups no more than two-thirds full.

Hard-Boiled Eggs and Avocado Toast

The pressure cooker is the best way to cook hard-boiled eggs—the shells peel easily and the eggs turn out perfect every time. Pair them with creamy avocado and cheese for a protein-packed breakfast. This recipe is easily customized to accommodate what you have on hand and can be made differently for you and your toddler.

MAKES 6 SERVINGS.

HARD-BOILED EGGS

6 large eggs

AVOCADO TOAST

½ avocado

Lemon juice, to taste

Sea salt, to taste

Freshly ground black pepper, to taste

Crushed red pepper flakes, to taste, optional

6 slices good multigrain bread with seeds

Olive oil or spreadable butter

¼ cup grated cheese (Cheddar [30 g] or Mozzarella [30 g]) or good melting cheese (Gruyere [30 g] or Brie [36 g])

1 *Prepare the hard-boiled eggs*: Pour 1 cup (235 ml) water into the pressure cooking pot and place a steamer basket in the bottom. Carefully place the eggs on the steamer basket. Lock the lid in place. Select High Pressure and 6 minutes cook time.

2 While the eggs are cooking, fill a bowl with ice and cold water. When the cook time ends, turn off the pressure cooker. Let the pressure release naturally for 6 minutes, then finish with a quick pressure release. When the float valve drops, carefully remove the lid.

3 Immediately put the eggs into the ice water to cool. Once cool, remove eggs from water and store in the refrigerator until ready to eat, up to 1 week.

4 *Prepare the toast:* In a medium bowl, mash the avocado, lemon juice, salt, pepper, and crushed red pepper flakes (if using).

5 Serve the toast one of two ways:

Open faced toast: Preheat the broiler. Toast the bread to your desired doneness, then drizzle a little olive oil on each slice. Spread the mashed avocado mixture on each piece of bread. Slice the hard-boiled eggs and layer on top, then add the cheese. Place on a baking sheet, then place under the broiler to melt the cheese, 1 to 2 minutes.

Toasted sandwich: Butter each slice of bread. Turn the bread over so the buttered side is facing down. Layer the avocado, egg, and cheese on three of the slices, then top with another slice of bread, buttered side facing up. Grill in a pan on the stove over medium heat. When one side is toasted, 2 to 3 minutes, flip and toast the opposite side for another 2 to 3 minutes. Slice in half to serve.

Tip

The perfect cook time for your eggs will depend on your altitude, brand of pressure cooker, and the thickness and material of your steamer basket. Some people prefer a 5-minute cook time and a 5-minute natural pressure release, while others prefer a 7-minute cook time and a 7-minute natural release. Experiment until you find your sweet spot.

If your toddler doesn't like eating big pieces of egg on their toast, you can use a cheese grater to grate the hard-boiled eggs. Combine the grated egg with the cheese and your toddler may not even notice it.

Chapter 7

Lunches for Toddlers

We've included several "three way" recipes that let you cook the protein one day and serve it three ways throughout the week. These lunch recipes are designed to minimize your cooking—serve your toddler different meats, sauces, and veggies separately, while you mix everything together and eat the finished dish for lunch.

Recipes

Diced Chicken Three Ways

Chicken breasts are so versatile! Spend a few minutes cooking one day and use the chicken for meals throughout the week. These three recipes offer a variety of flavors, colors, and textures that both you and your toddler will love.

MAKES 3 TO 4 CUPS (420 TO 560 G) COOKED CHICKEN, TO BE USED IN THE THREE RECIPES THAT FOLLOW.

3 large boneless, skinless chicken breasts, diced into bite-size pieces

½ teaspoon salt

½ teaspoon freshly ground black pepper

1 tablespoon (15 ml) vegetable oil

1 clove garlic, finely minced or pressed

1 cup (235 ml) reduced-sodium chicken broth

1 cup (185 g) rice

1¼ cups (285 ml) water

1 Select Sauté to preheat the pressure cooking pot. Season the diced chicken with salt and pepper. When the pot is hot, add the oil and chicken and sauté for 3 minutes. Add the galic and sauté for 1 minute more. Add the chicken broth and stir.

2 Place a trivet in the bottom of the pressure cooking pot. In a 7-inch (18 cm) cake pan, stir together the rice and water. Use a sling to lower the pan carefully onto the trivet. Lock the lid in place. Select High Pressure and 4 minutes cook time.

3 When the cook time ends, turn off the pressure cooker. Let the pressure release naturally for 7 minutes, then finish with a quick pressure release. When the float valve drops, carefully remove the lid. Use the sling to remove the pan from the pressure cooking pot and set the rice aside to use in the teriyaki chicken recipe that follows. Remove the trivet.

4 Transfer the chicken to a plate to cool and discard the cooking liquid. Divide the chicken into three equal portions.

Tip

We generally like to dice the chicken into adult-size bites to ensure the chicken doesn't cook too fast (and because it's tedious to cut all of the chicken breasts that small). Once the adult portion is dished up, use kitchen shears to cut the toddler portions of chicken into appropriately sized bites.

1 TERIYAKI BOWLS

MAKES 3 SERVINGS.

½ cup (60 g) cubed yellow squash (about ¼-inch [6 mm] cubes)

½ cup (60 g) cubed zucchini (about ¼-inch [6 mm] cubes)

¼ cup (30 g) matchstick carrots

½ cup (36 g) chopped broccoli florets

1 portion cooked cubed chicken (about 1 cup [140 g])

¼ cup (60 ml) teriyaki sauce

Cooked rice

Chili-garlic sauce, for serving, optional

Add 1 cup (235 ml) water to the pressure cooking pot. Place a steamer basket in the bottom of the cooking pot and add the squash, zucchini, carrots, and broccoli. Lock the lid in place. Select High Pressure and 0 minutes cook time. When the cook time ends, turn off the pressure cooker and use a quick pressure release. Carefully remove the steamer form the pot.

For the toddler: In a silicone baby food tray or small ice cube tray, fill each of the cups with a different food item—steamed veggies, cooked chicken, teriyaki sauce, rice, and diced fresh fruits.

For the parent: While the veggies steam, stir together the chicken and teriyaki sauce. To serve, top a scoop of white rice with the steamed vegetables and the teriyaki chicken mixture. Serve with chili-garlic sauce, if desired.

Tip

The teriyaki sauce you choose makes a big difference in the overall flavor of the dish. We prefer Kikkoman Teriyaki Sauce because it's not too spicy and has a great taste. Be sure to use your favorite.

2 STACKED GREEN ENCHILADAS

1 portion cooked cubed chicken (about 1 cup [140 g])

Four 4-inch (10 cm) corn or wheat tortillas

½ cup (120 ml) green enchilada sauce, (128 ml) green taco sauce, or (128 g) salsa verde, plus more for serving

1 cup (120 g) grated cheddar cheese

½ cup (90 g) grape tomatoes, quartered vertically

1 small can (2.25 ounces [63 g]) sliced olives, optional

1 avocado, peeled, pitted, and diced, for serving

Sour cream, for serving

1 tablespoon (1 g) chopped cilantro, optional

Nonstick cooking spray

For the toddler: In a silicone baby food tray or small ice cube tray, fill each of the cups with a different food item—cooked chicken, tortilla pieces, enchilada sauce, cheese, diced fresh fruits and vegetables, sour cream, and cilantro.

For the parent: Preheat the oven to 400°F (200°C, or gas mark 6). Spray a small oven-safe baking dish with nonstick cooking spray. Spoon a little enchilada sauce on the bottom of the dish. Place a tortilla on top of the enchilada sauce, and sprinkle on a thin layer of cheese, followed by half of the remaining diced chicken, then the enchilada sauce, then another thin layer of cheese. Top with another tortilla and repeat the layering process. Top with a final tortilla, the remaining enchilada sauce, and the remaining cheese. Place the dish in the oven and cook until the cheese is melted, bubbly, and just starting to brown, 5 to 10 minutes.

Remove from the oven and cool for 5 minutes. Serve topped with diced tomatoes, olives, avocado, sour cream, and cilantro.

Tip

If you like your enchiladas a little crisper, bake the tortillas in the oven until they start to brown, then sprinkle with cheese and return to the oven until melted.

3 CHICKEN SALAD SANDWICHES

1 portion cooked cubed chicken (about 1 cup [140 ml])

¼ cup (38 g) quartered grapes (sliced vertically)

¼ cup (30 g) diced celery

2 tablespoons (28 g) mayonnaise

2 tablespoons (30 g) sour cream

½ teaspoon fresh lemon juice

¼ teaspoon salt

¼ teaspoon freshly ground black pepper

1 tablespoon (6 g) sliced green onion, white and green parts

2 tablespoons (14 g) chopped pecans, toasted, optional

3 sandwich rolls or mini croissants, halved and toasted

For the toddler: In a silicone baby food tray or small ice cube tray, fill each of the cups with a different food item—cooked chicken, sliced grapes, diced celery, cubed sandwich rolls, and diced fresh fruits and vegetables.

For the parent: In a large bowl, stir together the mayonnaise, sour cream, lemon juice, salt, and pepper. Add the cooked chicken, grapes, celery, and green onion, and gently toss to combine. Cover and chill for at least 1 hour.

Just before serving, stir in the toasted pecans. Scoop the chicken salad mixture on toasted sandwich rolls or croissants.

Tip

For a lower carb option, you can serve this as a lettuce wrap.

Shredded Chicken Three Ways

Chicken cooked in the pressure cooker is tender, moist, and easy to shred. Here's how to cook shredded chicken in the pressure cooker and three great ways to serve it.

MAKES 3 TO 4 CUPS (420 TO 560 G) PREPARED CHICKEN, TO BE USED IN THE THREE RECIPES THAT FOLLOW.

3 large boneless, skinless chicken breasts

½ teaspoon salt

½ teaspoon freshly ground black pepper

1 tablespoon (15 ml) vegetable oil

1 clove garlic, finely minced or pressed

1 cup (235 ml) reduced-sodium chicken broth

1 Select Sauté to preheat the pressure cooking pot. Season the chicken with salt and pepper. When the pot is hot, add the oil and chicken and sauté for 1 to 2 minutes on each side. Add the garlic and sauté for 1 minute more, then add the chicken broth and stir. Lock the lid in place. Select High Pressure and 4 minutes cook time.

2 When the cook time ends, turn off the pressure cooker. Use a quick pressure release. When the float valve drops, carefully remove the lid.

3 Transfer the chicken to a plate to cool and reserve the cooking liquid. Shred the chicken and divide into three equal portions.

Tip

If frozen, add the chicken and 1 cup (235 ml) water or broth. Cook at High Pressure for 9 minutes, allow the pressure to release naturally for 5 minutes, then finish with a quick pressure release. (Use an instant-read thermometer to make sure the chicken is cooked through.)

1. BAKED CHICKEN TAQUITOS

MAKES 4 TAQUITOS.

1 portion cooked shredded chicken (about 1 cup [140 g])

1 can (14.5 ounces [410 g]) diced tomatoes with green chilies

¼ cup (64 g) green salsa, plus more for serving

½ teaspoon chili powder

¼ teaspoon onion powder

¼ teaspoon garlic powder

¼ teaspoon ground cumin

¼ teaspoon salt

¼ teaspoon freshly ground black pepper

2 teaspoons fresh lime juice

4 ounces (115 g) cream cheese, cubed

Four 6-inch (15 cm) flour tortillas

¾ cup (90 g) shredded Colby Jack cheese

1 tablespoon (1 g) fresh chopped cilantro

1 green onion, white and green parts, chopped

Nonstick cooking spray

Guacamole and/or sour cream, for serving, optional

For the toddler: In a silicone baby food tray or small ice cube tray, fill each of the cups with a different food item—shredded chicken, tomatoes, tortilla pieces, cheese, guacamole, sour cream, and diced fresh fruits and vegetables.

For the parent: Preheat the oven to 350°F (180°C, or gas mark 4). Line a baking sheet with parchment paper. In a small bowl, combine the diced tomatoes with green chilies, green salsa, chili powder, onion powder, garlic powder, cumin, salt, and pepper. Add the shredded chicken and stir until well combined. Select Sauté and cook uncovered for about 5 minutes, stirring occasionally, until all the liquid is absorbed. Stir in the lime juice. Adding a little at a time, stir in the cream cheese until melted.

Divide the chicken mixture among the tortillas. Top with the cheese, cilantro, and green onion. Tightly roll the tortilla around the filling. Place each taquito, seam-side down, on the prepared baking sheet. Spray the tops with cooking spray. Bake for 10 to 15 minutes, until crisp and golden brown on the ends, turning seam-side up halfway through the baking time. Serve with guacamole, green salsa, and sour cream, if desired.

Tip

If you prefer a softer tortilla, you can serve this warm out of the pressure cooker. Mix in your desired amount of Colby Jack cheese when you stir in the cream cheese. Fill your tortilla with the cheesy-chicken mixture and enjoy!

2. ASIAN LETTUCE WRAPS

1 cup (235 ml) reduced-sodium chicken broth

¼ cup (63 ml) hoisin sauce

2 tablespoons (28 ml) low-sodium soy sauce

¼ teaspoon chili-garlic sauce, plus more for serving

½ cup (93 g) white rice

¼ cup (31 g) canned sliced water chestnuts, drained and diced

½ cup (73 g) frozen diced carrots, thawed

1 portion cooked shredded chicken (about 1 cup [140 g])

1 green onion, white and green parts, sliced, optional

1 head butter lettuce, for serving

Sriracha, for serving, optional

For the toddler: In a silicone baby food tray or small ice cube tray, fill each of the cups with a different food item— shredded chicken, carrots, cooked rice, lettuce, and diced fresh fruits.

For the parent: In a small round pan, stir together the chicken broth, hoisin sauce, soy sauce, and chili-garlic sauce. Stir in the rice and water chestnuts. Pour 1 cup (235 ml) water into the pressure cooking pot and place a trivet in the bottom. Use a sling to lower the pan into the pressure cooker. Lock the lid in place. Select High Pressure and 4 minutes cook time.

When the cook time ends, turn off the pressure cooker. Let the pressure release naturally for 10 minutes, then finish with a quick pressure release. When the float valve drops, carefully remove the lid.

Use the sling to remove the pan from the pressure cooking pot. Add the carrots, shredded chicken, and sliced green onion. Stir well to combine. Serve wrapped in lettuce leaves topped with more chili-garlic sauce or Sriracha, if desired.

Tip

Even though the recipe calls for a small amount, the chili-garlic sauce gives this dish a great flavor, so we prefer to add it before cooking the rice. However, if it's too spicy for your toddler, feel free to omit it and mix a little into the parent portion before serving.

3. QUICK CHICKEN NOODLE SOUP

MAKES 3 SERVINGS.

1 tablespoon (14 g) unsalted butter

¼ cup (40 g) chopped onion

1 rib celery, chopped into ¼-inch (6 mm) pieces

2 carrots, peeled and chopped into ¼-inch (6 mm) pieces

1 clove garlic, minced

4 cups (946 ml) reduced-sodium chicken broth

1 teaspoon dried parsley

1 teaspoon salt

½ teaspoon freshly ground black pepper

1 sprig fresh thyme

1 portion cooked shredded chicken (about 1½ cups [210 g])

3 to 6 ounces (85 to 179 g) prepared egg noodles

Select Sauté on the pressure cooker and add the butter to the pressure cooking pot. When the butter is melted, add the onion, celery, carrots, and garlic, and sauté, stirring occasionally, until tender, about 2 minutes.

Add the broth, dried parsley, salt, pepper, and thyme. Lock the lid in place. Select High Pressure and 0 minutes cook time.

When the cook time ends, turn off the pressure cooker and use a quick pressure release. Carefully remove the lid. Remove the thyme sprig. Add the chicken and prepared egg noodles.

Tip

The recipe is written for vegetables cooked to crisp-tender. If you or your toddler prefers softer vegetables, increase the sauté time to 4 to 5 minutes.

Shredded Pork Three Ways

Pork shoulder cooks up tender and juicy in the pressure cooker and is a great base for lots of delicious meals. We prefer to combine the pork and seasonings for each of these meals while the pork is still hot and refrigerate the meals we're not eating so that the flavors can blend overnight.

MAKES 3 TO 4 CUPS (405 TO 540 G) SHREDDED PORK, TO BE USED IN THE THREE RECIPES THAT FOLLOW.

3 pounds (1.4 kg) pork shoulder, cut into 3 large pieces

1½ teaspoons kosher salt

½ teaspoon freshly ground black pepper

1 tablespoon (15 ml) vegetable oil

1 clove garlic, finely minced or pressed

1½ cups (355 ml) water

1 Select Sauté to preheat the pressure cooking pot. Season the pork with the salt and pepper. When the pot is hot, add the oil and pork and sauté for 3 minutes on each side. Add the garlic and sauté for 1 minute more. Add the water and stir, scraping up the browned bits on the bottom of the pan. Lock the lid in place. Select High Pressure and 75 minutes cook time.

2 When the cook time ends, turn off the pressure cooker. Allow the pressure to release naturally for 10 minutes, then finish with a quick pressure release. Carefully remove the lid.

3 Using a large fork or slotted spoon, carefully transfer the meat to a large platter and shred it with two forks. Discard any excess fat as you shred. If desired, use a fat separator to strain the juices in the cooking pot. Discard the fat and set the juices aside. Divide the pork into three equal portions.

Tip

I prefer to use pork shoulder roasts in the pressure cooker because pork sirloin roasts are leaner and don't cook up as tender.

1. PULLED PORK SANDWICHES

MAKES 3 OR 4 SANDWICHES.

1 portion cooked shredded pork (about 1 cup [135 g])

¼ cup (60 ml) reserved cooking liquid

¼ cup (65 ml) barbecue sauce, plus more for serving

3 or 4 sandwich rolls, toasted

For the toddler: In a silicone baby food tray or small ice cube tray, fill each of the cups with a different food item—cooked pork, barbecue sauce, cubed sandwich rolls, and diced fresh fruits and vegetables.

For the parent: In a small bowl, combine the reserved cooking liquid and barbecue sauce. Add the shredded pork and stir to combine. Serve on toasted rolls with more barbecue sauce, if desired.

Tip

You can mix the pork and reheat it in the microwave at 50 percent power for 1 minute at a time until it reaches the desired temperature.

2. QUICK CARNITAS STREET TACOS

MAKES 3 SERVINGS.

1 portion cooked shredded pork (about 1 cup [135 g])

¼ cup (60 ml) reserved cooking liquid

¼ teaspoon dried oregano

⅛ teaspoon ground cumin

½ teaspoon onion powder

½ teaspoon garlic powder

Salt and freshly ground black pepper

2 tablespoons (28 ml) fresh orange juice

Small 4-inch (10 cm) corn tortillas, guacamole, queso fresco, fresh chopped cilantro, lime juice, and sour cream, for serving

For the toddler: In a silicone baby food tray or small ice cube tray, fill each of the cups with a different food item—cooked pork, corn tortilla pieces, guacamole, queso fresco, sour cream, and diced fresh fruits and vegetables.

For the parent: Preheat the broiler. In a small bowl, combine the reserved cooking liquid, oregano, cumin, onion powder, garlic powder, salt, pepper, and orange juice. Add the pork and stir until well combined.

Line a rimmed baking sheet with aluminum foil and spread the shredded pork in a single layer. Broil for 3 to 5 minutes, or until the edges of the pork start to brown and crisp.

Serve in warmed tortillas topped with guacamole, queso fresco, cilantro, a squeeze of lime juice, and sour cream, as desired.

Tip

As your child grows you'll want to slowly start to introduce the spices you enjoy into their food as well.

3. KALUA PORK

MAKES 3 SERVINGS.

1 portion cooked shredded pork (about 1 cup [135 g])

½ cup (120 ml) reserved cooking liquid

1 to 2 teaspoons kosher salt, to taste

1 to 2 teaspoons liquid smoke, to taste

Cooked rice, steamed broccoli, carrot sticks, and fresh fruit (pineapple, mangoes), for serving

For the toddler: In a silicone baby food tray or small ice cube tray, fill each of the cups with a different food item—cooked pork, rice, broccoli, carrots, and diced fresh fruit.

For the parent: In a small bowl, combine the reserved cooking liquid, salt, and liquid smoke. Add the pork and stir until well combined.

Serve over cooked rice with a side of steamed broccoli, carrot sticks, and fresh fruit, as desired.

Tip

Start with less salt and liquid smoke and add more as desired.

Beef Strips Three Ways

Sirloin steak is a lean cut of beef that is quick cooking and versatile, and cooking it in the pressure cooker helps tenderize the meat.

MAKES ABOUT 4 CUPS (600 G) BEEF STRIPS, TO BE USED IN THE THREE RECIPES THAT FOLLOW.

3 pounds (1.4 kg) pork shoulder, cut into 3 large pieces

2 pounds (900 g) boneless beef sirloin steak, cut against the grain into ¼-inch (6 mm) thick slices

Salt and freshly ground black pepper

1 tablespoon (15 ml) vegetable oil, plus more as needed

½ cup (120 ml) reduced-sodium beef broth

½ teaspoon garlic powder

1 Select Sauté to preheat the pressure cooking pot. Season the beef strips with salt and pepper. Add the vegetable oil to the pressure cooking pot and quickly brown the beef strips on one side. Work in batches until all the meat is browned on one side. Add more oil if needed. Transfer the meat to a plate when browned.

2 Add the beef broth, garlic powder, ½ teaspoon salt, and ½ teaspoon pepper to the cooking pot and stir, scraping up the browned bits on the bottom of the pan. Return the browned beef to the pot.

3 Lock the lid in place. Select High Pressure and 12 minutes cook time. When the cook time ends, turn off the pressure cooker. Use a quick pressure release. Transfer the beef to a plate to cool and reserve the cooking liquid. Divide the beef into three equal portions.

Tip

The browning process makes a big difference in the flavor of the cooked beef, so if at all possible, don't skip this step.

1. ASIAN BEEF BOWLS

MAKES 3 SERVINGS.

1 portion cooked beef strips (about 1½ cups [225 g])

¼ cup (60 ml) reduced-sodium beef broth

¼ cup (60 ml) low-sodium soy sauce

1 tablespoon (15 g) packed light brown sugar

¼ teaspoon onion powder

¼ teaspoon garlic powder

2 teaspoons sesame oil

Dash of red pepper flakes

1 tablespoon (8 g) cornstarch

1 tablespoon (15 ml) cold water

1 cup (71 g) chopped broccoli, lightly steamed

Cooked rice and toasted sesame seeds, for serving

Tip

You can cook the sauce on the stovetop, if desired.

For the toddler: In a silicone baby food tray or small ice cube tray, fill each of the cups with a different food item—beef strips, steamed broccoli, soy sauce, and diced fresh fruit.

For the parent: In the pressure cooking pot, combine the beef broth, soy sauce, brown sugar, onion powder, garlic powder, sesame oil, and red pepper flakes, stirring until the sugar dissolves.

In a small bowl, whisk the cornstarch and 1 tablespoon (15 ml) cold water until smooth. Select Sauté and add the slurry to the pot, whisking constantly until the sauce comes to a boil and thickens. Stir in the beef strips and steamed broccoli.

Serve over cooked rice and garnish with toasted sesame seeds, if desired.

2. SMOTHERED BEEF BURRITOS

1 portion cooked beef strips (about 1½ cups [225 g])

¼ cup (60 ml) reduced-sodium beef broth

1 tablespoon (8 g) chili powder

¼ teaspoon smoked paprika

¼ teaspoon ground cumin

¼ teaspoon garlic powder

¼ teaspoon dried oregano

Salt and freshly ground pepper

3 burrito-size flour tortillas

Shredded cheese, Mexican rice, and black beans, for filling, optional

Enchilada sauce, sour cream, guacamole, and fresh salsa, for serving, optional

For the toddler: In a silicone baby food tray or small ice cube tray, fill each of the cups with a different food item—beef strips, cheese, Mexican rice, beans, sauce, guacamole, and diced fresh fruits and vegetables.

For the parent: Preheat the broiler. In the pressure cooking pot, combine the beef broth, chili powder, paprika, cumin, garlic powder, oregano, and salt and pepper to taste. Add the beef strips, select Sauté, and stir until the spices are incorporated and the beef is warmed through.

Use a slotted spoon to place ½ cup (75 g) warmed beef in the center of a tortilla and add shredded cheese and additional fillings of your choice. Fold in the edges and roll up tightly into a burrito. Repeat with the remaining tortillas. Top the burritos with your favorite enchilada sauce and more shredded cheese. Place on a baking sheet lined with parchment and broil for 2 to 4 minutes, until the cheese is bubbly. (Watch closely because the cheese browns quickly once it starts.) Serve topped with sour cream, guacamole, and fresh salsa, if desired.

Tip

Reheat the beef strips after mixing with the broth to keep the meat from drying out.

3. BEEF AND CHEDDAR SANDWICHES

MAKES 3 SANDWICHES.

1 tablespoon (14 g) unsalted butter
1 tablespoon (8 g) all-purpose flour
½ cup (120 ml) milk

Pinch of cayenne pepper, optional
Pinch of salt
¾ cup (90 g) shredded cheddar cheese

3 rolls or hamburger buns, toasted
1 portion cooked beef strips (about 1½ cups [225 g])

For the toddler: In a silicone baby food tray or small ice cube tray, fill each of the cups with a different food item—cheese sauce, diced buns, shredded beef, and diced fresh fruits and vegetables.

For the parent: In a small saucepan over medium heat, melt the butter. Sprinkle in the flour and cook until bubbling, stirring constantly. Gradually whisk in the milk, a little at a time, until the sauce is smooth and thick. Whisk in the cayenne and salt. Add the cheddar a handful at a time and stir until melted and smooth. Remove from the heat.

To serve, top each bun with warmed beef strips and ladle the cheese sauce on top.

Tip

If you'd prefer, replace the cayenne pepper with ½ to 1 teaspoon hot sauce (we used Frank's RedHot). It doesn't add much heat, but it does add a great flavor to the cheese sauce.

Ground Beef Three Ways

Ground beef is a staple in most families. It's relatively inexpensive and easy to find a flavor that everyone loves.

MAKES ABOUT 3 CUPS (675 G) GROUND BEEF, TO BE USED IN THE THREE RECIPES THAT FOLLOW.

2 pounds (900 g) ground beef

½ teaspoon salt

½ teaspoon freshly ground black pepper

1 tablespoon (15 ml) vegetable oil

1 clove garlic, finely minced or pressed

1½ cups (355 ml) reduced-sodium beef broth

Tip

Use a chopper spatula to help break up the ground beef while sautéing.

1 Select Sauté to preheat the pressure cooking pot. Season the ground beef with the salt and pepper. When the pot is hot, add the oil and ground beef and sauté for 3 minutes. Add the garlic and sauté for 1 minute more, then add the beef broth and stir. Lock the lid in place. Select High Pressure and 3 minutes cook time.

2 When the cook time ends, turn off the pressure cooker. Use a quick pressure release. When the float valve drops, carefully remove the lid.

3 Transfer the ground beef to a plate to cool and discard the cooking liquid. Divide the ground beef into three equal portions.

1. GROUND BEEF TACOS

MAKES 3 SERVINGS.

1 portion cooked ground beef (about 1 cup [225 g])

2 teaspoons chili powder

½ teaspoon ground cumin

½ teaspoon garlic powder

1 teaspoon onion powder

¼ teaspoon salt

Dash of cayenne pepper

Hard taco shells, lettuce, salsa, shredded cheese, diced tomatoes, and sour cream, for serving

Tip

If you'd prefer, you can substitute a tablespoon (8 g) of your favorite taco seasoning mix for the spices listed here.

For the toddler: In a silicone baby food tray or small ice cube tray, fill each of the cups with a different food item—cooked ground beef, shredded cheese, diced tomatoes, sour cream, and diced fresh fruits and vegetables.

For the parent: In a bowl, mix the beef, chili powder, cumin, garlic powder, onion powder, salt and cayenne pepper. Serve in hard taco shells with lettuce, salsa, shredded cheese, diced tomatoes, and sour cream.

2. LOADED BAKED POTATOES

MAKES 3 SERVINGS.

3 russet potatoes

2 tablespoons (28 g) unsalted butter

1 portion cooked ground beef (about 1 cup [225 g])

½ cup (36 g) steamed chopped broccoli

¼ cup (30 g) grated cheddar cheese

3 slices bacon, cooked and crumbled, optional

¼ cup (60 ml) ranch dressing or (60 ml) sour cream

1 teaspoon minced chives or thinly sliced green onions

1 cup (235 ml) water

Add 1 cup (235 ml) water to the pressure cooking pot and place a trivet in the bottom. Place the potatoes on the trivet. Lock the lid in place. Select High Pressure and 25 minutes cook time.

When the cook time ends, turn off the pressure cooker. Let the pressure release naturally for 5 minutes, then finish with a quick pressure release. When the float valve drops, carefully remove the lid. Use an instant-read thermometer to check that the potatoes reach 205°F (96°C) in the center. If needed, recover the pot and let them steam for a few minutes longer.

For the toddler: In a silicone baby food tray or small ice cube tray, fill each of the cups with a different food item—cooked ground beef, diced potato, broccoli, cheese, bacon, ranch dressing, and diced fresh fruits and vegetables.

For the parent: Slice the potatoes lengthwise and load them with butter, ground beef, broccoli, shredded cheese, and crumbled bacon. Drizzle with the ranch dressing and sprinkle with chives.

Tip

You can make this twice-baked or mashed-potato style; just scoop the potato out of the skins (leaving a little extra if you're doing twice-baked), then combine with milk, butter, and cheese. Mash together with a fork until well mixed. Spoon back into the potato skins, top with more cheese, and serve.

3. PASTA RAGU

MAKES 3 SERVINGS.

1 portion cooked ground beef (about 1 cup [225 g])

1½ cups (375 ml) marinara sauce, store-bought or homemade (page 160)

1 tablespoon (3 g) chopped fresh basil, optional

2½ cups (570 ml) water, plus more as needed

1 teaspoon salt

1 tablespoon (15 ml) vegetable oil

8 ounces (225 g) rotini pasta

Freshly grated Parmesan cheese, for serving

Tip

If you wish to substitute a different noodle, set your pressure cooker to cook at High Pressure for half the cook time on the package minus 1 minute.

For the toddler: In a silicone baby food tray or small ice cube tray, fill each of the cups with a different food item—ground beef, marinara sauce, pasta, cheese, and diced fresh fruits and vegetables.

For the parent: In a bowl, stir together the ground beef, marinara sauce, and fresh basil. Set aside.

Add the water, salt, vegetable oil, and pasta to the pressure cooking pot. If needed, add more water to just cover the pasta—do not stir. Lock the lid in place. Select High Pressure and 4 minutes cook time.

When the cook time ends, turn off the pressure cooker. Use a quick pressure release, or, if necessary, an intermittent pressure release. Ladle off any excess water from the pasta.

Serve the pasta topped with marinara sauce and freshly grated Parmesan cheese.

Chapter 8

Dinners for Toddlers

We have chosen not to cook separate meals for toddlers—we want them to start eating the foods and flavors the whole family enjoys. These dinner recipes are easily customized to be toddler-friendly while still representing a meal that parents are happy to eat.

Recipes

Crispy Chicken Fingers

These fresh chicken strips are breaded and baked—not fried—so they're a better-for-you meal you can feel good about enjoying with your toddler.

MAKES 4 SERVINGS.

1½ cups (168 g) panko (Japanese-style bread crumbs)

1 tablespoon (15 ml) olive oil

10 to 12 chicken tenders (1 to 1½ pounds [455 to 680 g])

2 to 3 teaspoons (12-18 g) salt, divided

1 teaspoon freshly ground black pepper, divided

½ cup (120 ml) chicken broth

½ cup (50 g) freshly grated Parmesan cheese

½ cup (63 g) all-purpose flour

½ teaspoon garlic powder

3 or 4 large egg whites

2 tablespoons (28 ml) water

Nonstick cooking spray

Ketchup or ranch dressing, for serving, optional

1 In a 12-inch (30 cm) skillet, stir together the panko and oil. Toast the panko over medium heat, stirring often, until golden, about 8 minutes. (Watch closely because the panko can burn quickly.) When toasted, spread the panko in a shallow dish to cool.

2 In the pressure cooking pot, combine the chicken tenders, 1 teaspoon salt, ½ teaspoon pepper, and chicken broth. Lock the lid in place. Select High Pressure and 2 minutes cook time.

3 When the cook time ends, turn off the pressure cooker. Allow the pressure to release naturally for 3 minutes, then finish with a quick pressure release. When the float valve drops, carefully remove the lid. Transfer the chicken to a paper towel-lined plate.

4 Adjust the oven rack to the middle position and preheat the oven to 475°F (240°C, or gas mark 9). In a first shallow dish, stir together the cooled panko and the grated Parmesan. In a second shallow dish, add the flour, garlic powder, remaining 1 to 2 teaspoons salt, and remaining ½ teaspoon pepper, and stir until well combined. In a third shallow dish, whisk together the egg whites and 2 tablespoons (28 ml) water.

5 Line a rimmed baking sheet with foil, place a wire rack on top, and spray the rack with a generous amount of nonstick cooking spray.

6 Lightly dredge each chicken tender in the egg whites, shaking off the excess. Dip in the flour mixture, shaking off the excess. Dip into the egg whites again, shaking off the excess. Finally, coat each chicken tender in the toasted panko, pressing the bread crumbs into the chicken strips to make sure they adhere. Lay the chicken on the wire rack.

7 Spray the tops of the chicken with nonstick cooking spray. Bake for 3 minutes, then flip and bake for 3 minutes more.

8 Serve with fresh fruits and vegetables, along with ketchup, ranch dressing, or another sauce for dipping.

Chicken Parmesan Variation

Add an extra teaspoon of garlic powder to the flour mixture. Prepare as directed. Bake at 475°F (240°C, or gas mark 9) for 3 minutes. Remove the chicken from the oven. Flip each piece of chicken and add marinara sauce, store-bought or homemade (page 160), and grated mozzarella cheese. Bake for 5 minutes longer, or until the cheese is melted. Serve over cooked pasta, topped with sauce and additional mozzarella and Parmesan cheese.

Tip

These breaded chicken strips freeze very well! If you want, you can cook up a double or triple batch. (You may need to add another minute to the cook time.) After baking, allow to cool to room temperature. In a freezer-safe ziplock bag, lay the chicken strips flat, separated by parchment paper. When ready to cook, take directly from the freezer to a preheated oven and cook at 400°F (200°C, or gas mark 6) for 5 to 10 minutes, checking periodically.

Cheesy Potatoes

Always a hit at any meal, these ooey-gooey cheesy potatoes have a crisp buttery topping that you and your toddler will love.

MAKES 4 SERVINGS.

5 tablespoons (70 g) unsalted butter, divided

¼ cup (40 g) chopped onion

1 cup (235 ml) reduced-sodium chicken broth

1 teaspoon salt

¼ teaspoon freshly ground black pepper

1 bag (20 ounces [560 g]) shredded fresh hashbrown potatoes

Nonstick cooking spray

1 cup (112 g) panko bread crumbs

⅓ cup (77 g) sour cream

1 cup (115 g) shredded Monterey Jack cheese

Tip

If you like, substitute the shredded potatoes with five potatoes, thinly sliced, and increase the cook time by 2 minutes.

1 Select Sauté and melt 2 tablespoons (28 g) butter in the pressure cooking pot. Add the onion. Sauté for about 3 minutes, stirring occasionally, until tender. Add the chicken broth, salt, and pepper. Put the steamer basket in the cooking pot and add the potatoes. Lock the lid in place. Select High Pressure and 3 minutes cook time.

2 While the potatoes cook, preheat the broiler. Spray a 9 x 13-inch (23 x 33 cm) ovenproof dish with nonstick cooking spray. In a small microwave-safe bowl, melt the remaining 3 tablespoons (42 g) butter and stir in the panko. Set aside.

3 When the cook time ends, turn off the pressure cooker and use a quick pressure release. When the float valve drops, carefully remove the lid. Remove the steamer basket with the potatoes and transfer the potatoes to the prepared dish.

4 Stir the sour cream and Monterey Jack cheese into the cooking liquid in the pot and pour the mixture over the potatoes. Use two forks to gently mix the sauce with the potatoes. Top with the panko topping and broil for 5 to 7 minutes, or until golden brown.

Broccoli Cheesy Chicken and Rice

Layered pot-in-pot cooking in the pressure cooker allows you to cook your whole dinner at the same time. In this dish, the rice cooks in a separate pot right on top of the chicken.

1 large boneless, skinless chicken breast, cut into bite-size pieces

Salt and freshly ground black pepper

1 tablespoon (15 ml) olive oil

¼ cup (40 g) chopped onion

1 tablespoon (14 g) unsalted butter

1 cup (235 ml) reduced-sodium chicken broth

¼ teaspoon salt

¼ teaspoon pepper

2 teaspoons dried parsley

1 cup (185 g) white rice

1¼ cups (285 ml) water

2 tablespoons (16 g) cornstarch

2 tablespoons (28 ml) cold water

2 ounces (55 g) cream cheese, cut into cubes

½ cup (58 g) shredded cheddar cheese, plus more for garnishing

1 cup (71 g) chopped broccoli, lightly steamed, for serving

Red pepper flakes, optional

1 Season the chicken with salt and pepper to taste. Select Sauté to preheat the pressure cooking pot. When hot, add the olive oil and the onion and sauté for 1 minute. Add the diced chicken and butter and sauté for 2 minutes more. Stir in the broth, ¼ teaspoon salt, ¼ teaspoon pepper, and the parsley.

2 Place a trivet in the bottom of the pressure cooking pot over the chicken. In a 7-inch (18 cm) cake pan, stir together the rice and 1¼ cups (285 ml) water. Use a sling to lower the pan carefully onto the trivet. Lock the lid in place. Select High Pressure and 4 minutes cook time.

3 When the cook time ends, turn off the pressure cooker. Allow the pressure to release naturally for 10 minutes, then use a quick pressure release. When the float valve drops, carefully remove the lid.

4 Use the sling to remove the pan from the cooking pot. Remove the trivet. (If your toddler doesn't like sauce on their meat, use a slotted spoon to remove their chicken to a bowl and set aside.)

5 In a small bowl, whisk the cornstarch and 2 tablespoons (28 ml) cold water until smooth. Select Sauté and add the slurry to the pot, stirring constantly. Add the cream cheese and cheddar cheese, stirring until melted.

6 Serve the cheesy chicken over the rice and steamed broccoli and garnish with more cheddar cheese, if desired. Season with additional salt, black pepper, or red pepper flakes to taste.

Tip

You can steam the broccoli in the pressure cooker if you prefer. After pressure cooking, remove the rice from the cake pan to a serving bowl. Place the broccoli in the cake pan and return the pan to the cooking pot. Replace the lid and allow the broccoli to steam in the cooking pot until fork-tender, 2 to 4 minutes. Remove the cake pan and trivet and continue with the recipe as directed.

Fiesta Chicken Salad

If salads are a little too adventurous for your toddler, you can serve the chicken and rice mixture in a taco shell, using the homemade salad dressing as a dip.

MAKES 4 SERVINGS.

CILANTRO-LIME DRESSING

3 tablespoons (32 g) Hidden Valley Ranch Dressing Mix

1 cup (225 g) mayonnaise

½ cup (120 ml) milk or buttermilk

1 tablespoon (15 ml) fresh lime juice

2 cloves garlic, minced or pressed

½ cup (8 g) chopped fresh cilantro

¼ cup (64 g) mild green salsa

¼ teaspoon red pepper flakes, optional

CILANTRO LIME CHICKEN AND RICE

1 tablespoon (15 ml) extra virgin olive oil

1 pound (455 g) ground chicken

2 tablespoons (20 g) finely chopped onion

1 cup (235 ml) reduced-sodium chicken broth

½ cup (93 g) long-grain white rice

1 teaspoon salt

½ teaspoon ground cumin

¼ teaspoon black pepper

1 can (10 ounces [280 g]) diced tomatoes with green chilies (Rotel Mild)

1 tablespoon (15 ml) fresh lime juice

1 tablespoon (8 g) cornstarch

1 tablespoon (15 ml) cold water

¼ cup (4 g) chopped fresh cilantro

1 can (14.5 ounces [410 g]) black beans, drained and rinsed

2 cups (94 g) shredded romaine

1 cup (180 g) chopped tomatoes, for serving, optional

1 avocado, peeled, pitted, and diced, for serving, optional

Shredded cheddar cheese, for serving

1 *Prepare the dressing:* In a blender jar, combine ranch dressing mix, mayonnaise, milk, lime juice, garlic, cilantro, green salsa, and red pepper flakes (if using). Pulse until well combined. Refrigerate for several hours or overnight.

2 *Prepare the chicken and rice:* Select Sauté to preheat the pressure cooking pot. When the pot is hot, add the olive oil and chicken. Cook for about 5 minutes, crumbling with a spoon, until browned. Add the onion and cook for 1 minute more, stirring frequently. Stir in the chicken broth, rice, salt, cumin, black pepper, diced tomatoes with green chilies, and lime juice. Lock the lid in place.

Select High Pressure and 4 minutes cook time.

3 When the cook time ends, turn off the pressure cooker. Let the pressure release naturally for 10 minutes, then finish with a quick pressure release. When the float valve drops, carefully remove the lid.

4 In a small bowl, whisk the cornstarch and cold water until smooth. Add the slurry to the pot. Select Sauté and cook, stirring constantly, until the sauce reaches your desired thickness. Stir in the cilantro and beans.

5 Serve over lettuce, with tomatoes, avocado, and cheese and a drizzle of cilantro-lime dressing on top.

Tip

The cilantro-lime dressing keeps in the refrigerator for up to 2 weeks, and we love to drizzle a little over tacos or vegetables, or even use it as a chip dip.

Creamy Cashew Chicken and Broccoli

Based on an award-wining recipe, the whole family will love this cashew chicken cooked with a hint of rosemary and drizzled in rich Gouda cheese.

MAKES 4 SERVINGS.

CASHEW CHICKEN

1 tablespoon (15 ml) olive oil

¼ cup (40 g) finely diced red onion

1 tablespoon (14 g) unsalted butter

2 large boneless, skinless chicken breasts (about 1 pound [455 g]), diced into bite-size pieces

½ cup (120 ml) reduced-sodium chicken broth

½ teaspoon crushed rosemary leaves

1 cup (185 g) white rice

1¼ cups (285 ml) water

2 tablespoons (16 g) cornstarch

2 tablespoons (28 ml) cold water

½ cup (70 g) cashews, coarsely chopped

1 cup (71 g) chopped broccoli, lightly steamed, for serving

GOUDA CREAM SAUCE

2 tablespoons (28 g) unsalted butter

2 tablespoons (16 g) all-purpose flour

1 cup (235 ml) half-and-half, plus more if needed

5 slices Gouda cheese

Salt and freshly ground black pepper

1 *Prepare the cashew chicken:* Select Sauté to preheat the pressure cooking pot. When the pot is hot, add the olive oil and onion to the cooking pot and sauté for 1 minute. Add 1 tablespoon (28 g) butter and the diced chicken, and sauté for 2 minutes more. Add the chicken broth and rosemary.

2 Place a trivet in the bottom of the pressure cooking pot over the chicken. In a 7-inch (18 cm) cake pan, stir together the rice and 1¼ cups (285 ml) water. Use a sling to lower the pan carefully onto the trivet. Lock the lid in place. Select High Pressure and 4 minutes cook time.

3 *Prepare the Gouda cream sauce:* While the chicken and rice are cooking, in a small saucepan on the stovetop over medium heat, melt the 2 tablespoons (28 g) butter. Whisk in the flour.

Cook for 2 to 3 minutes, stirring constantly, until smooth and bubbly. Gradually add the half-and-half, stirring constantly, until the sauce is thick and smooth, about 2 minutes. Reduce the heat to low and add the Gouda cheese, a little at a time, until smooth and creamy. Add more half-and-half, if necessary, to thin the sauce to the desired consistency. Season with salt and pepper to taste. Remove from the heat. (If your pressure cooker can sauté on a low heat setting, you can choose to do this step in your pressure cooker.)

4 When the cook time ends, turn off the pressure cooker. Allow the pressure to release naturally for 10 minutes, then use a quick pressure release. When the float valve drops, carefully remove the lid. Use the sling to remove the cake pan and set aside. Remove the trivet.

Tip

If you don't have red onions on hand, you can substitute white or yellow onions.

5 In a small bowl, mix the cornstarch and 2 tablespoons (28 ml) cold water until smooth. Select Sauté and add the slurry to the pot and cook, stirring constantly, until the liquid thickens. Stir in ½ cup (120 ml) of the Gouda cream sauce and the cashews.

6 Serve the chicken over the rice and steamed broccoli, topped with extra Gouda cream sauce.

Deconstructed Chicken Pot Pie

This toddler spin on classic chicken pot pie features a thicker, easier-to-eat sauce and fun pie dough cutouts that your toddler can pick up and eat with their fingers.

MAKES 4 SERVINGS.

1 piecrust, store-bought or homemade (recipe follows)

1 tablespoon (15 ml) vegetable oil

½ cup (80 g) diced onion

1 rib celery, chopped

½ cup (120 ml) reduced-sodium chicken broth

2 large boneless, skinless chicken breasts (about 1 pound [455 g]), diced into bite-size pieces

1 large russet potato, cut into 1-inch (2.5 cm) cubes

½ teaspoon salt

¼ teaspoon freshly ground black pepper

1 cup (140 g) frozen carrots and peas, steamed

⅓ cup (75 g) unsalted butter

⅓ cup (42 g) all-purpose flour

½ cup (120 ml) milk, plus more as needed

1 Preheat the oven to 425°F (220°C, or gas mark 7). Line a baking sheet with parchment paper (or spray with nonstick cooking spray) and set aside. Roll out the piecrust dough to ⅛ inch (3 mm) thick. Use cookie cutters to create shapes in the piecrust and transfer to the baking sheet. Bake according to the package directions until lightly browned. Remove from the oven and allow to cool.

2 Select Sauté to preheat the pressure cooking pot. When hot, add the vegetable oil, onion, and celery. Sauté for about 3 minutes, stirring occasionally, until the onion is tender. Stir in the chicken broth, diced chicken, potato, salt, and pepper. Lock the lid in place. Select High Pressure and 4 minutes cook time.

3 When the cook time ends, turn off the pressure cooker. Use a quick pressure release. When the float valve drops, carefully remove the lid. Stir in the carrots and peas.

4 In a small saucepan on the stovetop over medium heat, melt the butter. Whisk in the flour. Cook for 2 to 3 minutes, stirring constantly, until smooth and bubbly. Gradually add the milk, stirring constantly for about 2 minutes, until the sauce is thick and smooth. Add this to the pressure cooking pot and stir until the sauce is thick and creamy. Add more milk, if needed, to achieve your desired consistency.

5 To serve, place the cooked pot pie filling into individual bowls and top with the piecrust shapes.

Tip

Most toddlers love using the cookie cutters to help cut out the piecrust pieces. However, because toddlers don't have the best sense of where to position the cookie cutter, you can let them have their turn first and then use a knife to cut the leftover crust into shapes and bake it all up at once.

HOMEMADE PIE CRUST

1¼ cups (156 g) all-purpose flour, plus more for rolling the dough
½ teaspoon salt
2 tablespoons (28 g) unsalted butter, chilled
⅓ cup (75 g) shortening, chilled (we prefer butter-flavored shortening)
3 tablespoons (45 ml) ice water

1 In a large bowl, combine the flour and salt. Cut the butter and shortening into small cubes and add them to the flour mixture. Use a pastry cutter or two knives to cut the butter and shortening into the flour until it resembles very coarse meal.

2 One tablespoon (15 ml) at a time, add the water to the dough, mixing it in with a fork. Add just enough water so the dough holds together when you squeeze a handful. (It will still look dry and crumbly.) Form the dough into a round disk and wrap it in plastic wrap. Chill for 30 minutes.

3 On a well-floured surface, roll the dough into a 12-inch (30 cm) circle that's ⅛ inch (3 mm) thick. Use the cookie cutters to cut out fun shapes, then bake at 425°F (220°C, or gas mark 7) for 15 to 20 minutes until lightly browned.

Buttery Spiced Chicken and Noodles

This is another great one-pot meal! The spaghetti cooks on the bottom while the chicken cooks on the top—coated in spices and browned in butter. After cooking, the chicken is made into in a rich, colorful cream sauce to serve on top of the pasta.

MAKES 4 SERVINGS.

Nonstick cooking spray
1 teaspoon garlic powder
½ teaspoon onion powder
½ teaspoon chili powder
½ teaspoon paprika
½ teaspoon salt

¼ teaspoon black pepper
1 pound (455 g) chicken tenders (about 6 strips)
1 tablespoon (14 g) unsalted butter
1 tablespoon (15 ml) vegetable oil
¼ cup (60 ml) reduced-sodium chicken broth

6 ounces (170 g) spaghetti, broken in half
2 cups (475 ml) water
1 tablespoon (8 g) cornstarch
1 tablespoon (15 ml) cold water
1 cup (235 ml) heavy cream
1 tablespoon (1 g) dried parsley

1 Coat a 7-inch (18 cm) cake pan with nonstick cooking spray. Set aside.

2 In a mixing bowl, combine the garlic powder, onion powder, chili powder, paprika, salt, and pepper. Add the chicken and toss with your hands to coat the chicken with the spices.

3 Select Sauté and preheat the pressure cooking pot. When the pot is hot, add the butter and oil and stir until the butter is melted. Add the chicken and sauté on both sides, about 2 minutes per side. Remove the chicken to the prepared cake pan. Pour the chicken broth into the cooking pot to deglaze the pan. Scrape the browned bits off of the bottom of the pan and pour over the chicken in the cake pan. Wipe out the cooking pot with a paper towel.

4 Place the spaghetti in the pressure cooking pot. Pour in enough water to just cover the spaghetti noodles, about 2 cups (475 ml). Place a tall trivet in the cooking pot over the spaghetti and use a sling to lower the cake pan carefully on top. Lock the lid in place. Select High Pressure and 4 minutes cook time.

5 When the cook time ends, turn off the pressure cooker. Allow the pressure to release naturally for 2 minutes, then use a quick pressure release. When the float valve drops, carefully remove the lid.

6 Use the sling to carefully remove the cake pan from the cooking pot. Remove the trivet. Pour the spaghetti into a strainer to drain. Return the contents of the cake pan to the pressure cooking pot. (If your toddler doesn't like sauce on their chicken, use a slotted spoon to remove their portion to a bowl and set aside.)

Tip

When you're in a hurry, you can place the chicken and spices in a ziplock bag and shake to evenly coat the chicken.

7 In a small bowl, dissolve the cornstarch in the 1 tablespoon (15 ml) cold water. Push the chicken to one side of the cooking pot and add the cornstarch slurry. Select Sauté and cook, stirring constantly, until the sauce thickens. Turn off the pressure cooker and stir in the heavy cream and parsley.

8 Serve the chicken and sauce over the spaghetti noodles along with your toddler's favorite vegetables.

Sweet Asian Chicken and Rice

Kids love this mild, sweet honey sauce, so this meal is likely to become part of your regular rotation. The sesame oil is the secret ingredient that makes this dish; even though it's just a small amount, don't skip it!

MAKES 4 SERVINGS.

2 large boneless, skinless chicken breasts (about 1 pound [455 g]), diced

Salt and freshly ground black pepper

1 tablespoon (15 ml) vegetable oil

¼ cup (40 g) diced onion

1 clove garlic, minced

¼ cup (60 ml) low-sodium soy sauce

¼ cup (31 g) chopped water chestnuts

1 tablespoon (16 g) tomato paste

⅛ teaspoon red pepper flakes

1 cup (185 g) white rice

1¼ cups (285 ml) water

1 teaspoon sesame oil

¼ cup (85 g) honey

1 tablespoon (8 g) cornstarch

1 tablespoon (15 ml) cold water

1 green onion, white and green parts, chopped

Tip

If you want this to be a one-pot meal complete with veggies, add frozen peas or fresh snap peas to the pot when after you add the cornstarch slurry and allow to warm through.

1 Season the chicken with salt and pepper. Select Sauté to preheat the pressure cooking pot. When the pot is hot, add the vegetable oil, onion, garlic, and chicken. Sauté for about 3 minutes, stirring occasionally, until the onion softens. Stir in the soy sauce, water chestnuts, tomato paste, and red pepper flakes.

2 Place a trivet in the bottom of the pressure cooking pot over the chicken. In a 7-inch (18 cm) cake pan, stir together the rice and water. Use a sling to lower the pan carefully onto the trivet. Lock the lid in place. Select High Pressure and 4 minutes cook time.

3 When the cook time ends, turn off the pressure cooker. Allow the pressure to release naturally for 7 minutes, then use a quick pressure release. When the float valve drops, carefully remove the lid. Use the sling to remove the pan from the cooking pot. Remove the trivet.

4 Add the sesame oil and honey to the pot and stir to combine.

5 In a small bowl, whisk the cornstarch and cold water until smooth. Add the slurry to the pot. Select Sauté and simmer, stirring constantly, until the sauce thickens. Stir in the green onions. Serve over the rice.

Bow Tie Pasta with Chicken Alfredo Sauce

So many kids love Alfredo sauce. This quick-and-easy recipe cooks the pasta and the chicken together in the pressure cooker, so it's ready in less than 30 minutes.

MAKES 4 SERVINGS.

1 large boneless, skinless chicken breast, diced into bite-size pieces

Salt and freshly ground black pepper

2 tablespoons (28 g) unsalted butter

1 clove garlic, minced or pressed

2½ cups (570 ml) water

½ teaspoon salt

8 ounces (225 g) bow tie pasta (farfalle)

½ cup (50 g) grated Parmesan cheese, plus more for serving

½ cup (120 ml) heavy cream

2 tablespoons (16 g) cornstarch

2 tablespoons (28 ml) cold water

1 tablespoon (4 g) chopped fresh parsley, optional

1 Lightly season the diced chicken with salt and pepper. Select Sauté to preheat the pressure cooking pot. When the pot is hot, add the butter to melt. Add the chicken and sauté for 3 minutes, stirring occasionally. Add the garlic and sauté for 1 minute more.

2 Add the 2½ cups (570 ml) water and salt to the pressure cooking pot, then stir in the bow tie pasta. Lock the lid in place. Select High Pressure and 4 minutes cook time.

3 When the cook time ends, turn off the pressure cooker and allow the pressure to release naturally for 3 minutes, then finish with a quick pressure release. (If foam or liquids begin to come from the steam release valve, close it and wait a minute, then try again.) When the float valve drops, carefully remove the lid.

4 Turn off the pressure cooker. Add the Parmesan cheese and stir until melted. Stir in the heavy cream. In a small bowl, combine the cornstarch and 2 tablespoons (28 ml) cold water and mix well. Select Sauté, pour in the slurry, and simmer, stirring occasionally, until the sauce has thickened and the pasta is tender, 2 to 3 minutes.

5 Remove the pressure cooking pot from the housing to cool. The sauce will continue to thicken as it cools. (When reheating, you'll need to stir in a little milk to return the sauce to full creaminess.)

6 If your toddler doesn't object to green, stir in the parsley for added color. Scoop into individual bowls, and season with additional salt, black pepper, or Parmesan to taste.

Tip

Omit the chicken if you are looking for a meatless meal or stir in frozen chopped veggies and allow them to warm through to pump up the nutrition.

Creamy Chicken Pesto Pasta

Known as "green mac and cheese" at our house, this pasta is loaded with fresh vegetables! Using prepared pesto makes this meal come together in a flash!

1 tablespoon (14 g) unsalted butter

1 clove garlic, minced

1 large boneless, skinless chicken breast, cut into bite-size pieces

1 cup (235 ml) reduced-sodium chicken broth

1 cup (235 ml) water

8 ounces (225 g) rotini pasta

½ teaspoon salt, plus more as needed

¼ teaspoon freshly ground black pepper, plus more as needed

2 ounces (55 g) cream cheese, cubed

2 tablespoons (28 ml) milk

1 tablespoon (15 g) prepared pesto

1 cup (124 g) frozen green beans, thawed

½ cup (75 g) grape tomatoes, quartered vertically

1 tablespoon finely chopped fresh (3 g) basil or (4 g) parsley, for serving, optional

Freshly grated mozzarella or Parmesan cheese, for serving

1 Select Sauté to preheat the pressure cooking pot. When the pot is hot, add the butter to melt. Stir in the garlic and cook for 30 seconds. Add the chicken and sauté for 3 minutes, stirring occasionally. Stir in the chicken broth, water, rotini, salt, and pepper. Lock the lid in place. Select High Pressure and 4 minutes cook time.

2 When the cook time ends, turn off the pressure cooker. Let the pressure release naturally for 3 minutes, then finish with a quick pressure release. When the float valve drops, carefully remove the lid.

3 Stir the cream cheese into the hot pasta until melted. Stir in the milk and pesto until blended. Stir in the green beans and cover the pot to steam for 2 minutes, or until the green beans are crisp-tender. Mix in the tomatoes and season with salt and pepper to taste.

4 Serve topped with basil and grated mozzarella.

Tip

Although the pesto flavor of this dish is quite mild, for picky toddlers, you can pull out the chicken and pasta right after pressure cooking or after stirring in the milk and cream cheese. You can also substitute your child's favorite vegetable in place of the green beans.

Macaroni and Cheese with Chicken and Vegetables

Mac and cheese is a classic kid favorite! Feel better about serving it to your toddler by adding chicken and veggies.

MAKES 4 SERVINGS

1 large boneless, skinless chicken breast, cut into bite-size pieces

Salt and freshly ground black pepper

1 tablespoon (15 ml) vegetable oil

2 cups (475 ml) water

1 teaspoon salt

1 teaspoon ground mustard

8 ounces (225 g) elbow macaroni

1 can (12 ounces [340 g]) evaporated milk

2 cups (225 g) shredded mild cheddar cheese

½ cup (70 g) frozen diced vegetables, such as peas and carrots

Cayenne pepper, Sriracha, or red pepper flakes, for serving, optional

1 Season the diced chicken with salt and pepper. Select Sauté to preheat the pressure cooking pot. When hot, add the vegetable oil and diced chicken. Sauté for 3 minutes, stirring occasionally.

2 Add the water, salt, and ground mustard to the pressure cooking pot. Stir in the elbow macaroni. Lock the lid in place. Select High Pressure and 4 minutes cook time.

3 When the cook time ends, turn off the pressure cooker and allow the pressure to release naturally for 3 minutes, then finish with a quick pressure release. (If foam or liquid begins to come from the steam release valve, close it and wait a minute, then try again.) When the float valve drops, carefully remove the lid.

4 Stir in the evaporated milk. Select Sauté and simmer, stirring occasionally, until the pasta is tender, 2 to 3 minutes. (It still might look like too much liquid is in the pot, but it will continue to thicken as it cools.)

5 Turn off the pressure cooker. Add a handful of cheddar cheese and stir until the cheese has melted and the sauce is smooth. Repeat this process one handful at a time until all the cheese is melted and the sauce is smooth. (Adding the cheese all at once will cause the cheese to clump together.)

6 Add the frozen diced vegetables and stir until well combined. Cover with the lid until the vegetables are warmed through, about 3 minutes.

7 Remove the pressure cooking pot from the housing to cool. (When reheating, you'll need to stir in a little milk to return the mac and cheese to full creaminess.) Season with additional salt, black pepper, cayenne pepper, Sriracha, or red pepper flakes to taste.

Tip

Bacon is a nice addition to the parent portion. Simply dice the bacon, then add it to the pressure cooking pot. Select Sauté and cook, stirring occasionally, until the bacon is crisp. Use a slotted spoon to quickly remove the bacon to a paper towel–lined plate. Then sauté the diced chicken in the remaining bacon fat, adding up to 1 tablespoon (15 ml) of oil as needed. Continue with the recipe as directed, and sprinkle on the crisp bacon just prior to serving.

Hearty Potato Cheese Soup

This is one of the most popular recipes on *Pressure Cooking Today*—everyone loves the chunky potatoes and the creamy soup! We've thickened the broth and cut the potatoes bite-size so it's a toddler-friendly meal that you'll look forward to eating, too.

MAKES 4 SERVINGS.

1 tablespoon (14 g) plus ⅓ cup (75 g) unsalted butter, divided

¼ cup (40 g) chopped onion

1 can (14.5 ounces [410 g]) chicken broth

½ teaspoon salt

¼ teaspoon black pepper

Dash of red pepper flakes

1 tablespoon (1 g) dried parsley

3 cups (330 g) peeled and cubed potatoes

2 ounces (55 g) cream cheese, cubed

½ cup (58 g) shredded cheddar cheese

1 cup (235 ml) half-and-half

½ cup (82 g) frozen corn

4 slices crisp-cooked bacon, crumbled

⅓ cup (42 g) all-purpose flour

½ cup (120 ml) milk, plus more as needed

Tip

The butter-flour-milk mixture, known as a roux, thickens this soup quite a bit. If you prefer, you can omit it entirely or keep it separate and stir some into your toddler's soup until their portion reaches the desired thickness.

1 Select Sauté to preheat the pressure cooking pot. When the pot is hot, add 1 tablespoon (14 g) butter to melt. Add the onion and cook, stirring occasionally, until tender, about 2 minutes. Add the chicken broth, salt, pepper, red pepper flakes, and parsley and stir to combine.

2 Put the steamer basket in the pressure cooking pot over the broth. Add the cubed potatoes. Lock the lid in place. Select High Pressure and 4 minutes cook time.

3 When the cook time ends, turn off the pressure cooker. Allow the pressure to release naturally for 5 minutes, then finish with a quick pressure release. When the float valve drops, carefully remove the potatoes and steamer basket from the pressure cooking pot.

4 Add the cream cheese and shredded cheese to the liquid in the pot. Stir until the cheese is melted. Add half-and-half, corn, crumbled bacon, and cooked potatoes, and heat through but do not bring to a boil.

5 In a small saucepan on the stovetop over medium heat, melt the remaining ⅓ cup (75 g) butter. Whisk in the flour. Cook for 2 to 3 minutes, stirring constantly, until smooth and bubbly. Gradually add the milk, stirring constantly, and cook for about 2 minutes, until the sauce is thick and smooth. Add this to the pressure cooking pot and stir until the soup is thick and creamy. Add more milk or broth, if needed, to achieve your desired consistency.

Sauce-Separate Lasagna

The sauce in this recipe is made separately in case your toddler is picky. Cottage cheese has a milder flavor than ricotta and a higher moisture content, making it perfect for this sauce-separate lasagna recipe.

MAKES 4 SERVINGS.

8 ounces (225 g) country-style sausage

1 can (14.5 ounces [410 g]) diced tomatoes, well drained

1 can (8 ounces [225 g]) tomato sauce

1 teaspoon garlic powder

1 teaspoon dried basil

⅛ teaspoon red pepper flakes

¼ teaspoon salt

1 cup (225 g) plus 3 tablespoons (42 g) cottage cheese, divided

1½ cups (173 g) shredded Mozzarella cheese, divided

½ cup (40 g) shredded Parmesan cheese

Nonstick cooking spray

6 no-boil lasagna noodles

1 Select Sauté to preheat the pressure cooking pot. When the pot is hot, add the sausage. Cook for about 5 minutes, stirring frequently to break up the meat, until the sausage is no longer pink. Drain any excess fat from the pot. Stir in the tomatoes, tomato sauce, garlic powder, basil, red pepper flakes, and salt. Transfer to the top stackable stainless steel pan and set aside. Wipe out the pressure cooking pot.

2 In a large bowl, mix together 1 cup (225 g) cottage cheese, 1 cup (115 g) Mozzarella, and the Parmesan until blended. Spray the bottom stackable stainless steel pan with nonstick cooking spray. Spread the remaining 3 tablespoons (42 g) cottage cheese on the bottom of the prepared pan. Break the noodles into pieces to form a single layer on top of the cottage cheese. Spread half of the cheese mixture on top of the noodles. Add a second layer of noodles and the remaining cheese mixture. Top with a third layer of noodles and sprinkle with the remaining ½ cup (60 g) mozzarella.

3 Add 1 cup (235 ml) water to the cooking pot. Place the double-stack pan in the pot. Lock the lid in place. Select High Pressure and 20 minutes cook time.

4 When the cook time ends, turn off the pressure cooker. Let the pressure release naturally for 10 minutes, then finish with a quick pressure release. When the float valve drops, carefully remove the lid. Remove the pan from the cooking pot and let rest for 5 minutes prior to serving.

Tip

If you want to prepare the sauce on the stovetop, you can double the recipe and cook lasagna in both the top and the bottom stacked pans. If you don't have a stackable stainless steel cooking pan, you can cook the sauce on the bottom of the pressure cooking pot and pre-pare the lasagna in a 7-inch (18 cm) cake pan. Place the cake pan on a trivet directly above the sauce and cook as directed.

Rotini with Meatless Marinara Sauce

Kids will often try sauces if you give them a separate bowl filled with sauce for them to dip their noodles into, so this recipe cooks the sauce in a separate bowl on top of your pasta. Some toddlers are picky about having meat in their pasta sauce; however, if your toddler likes meat sauce, add some browned ground beef.

MAKES 4 SERVINGS.

2½ cups (570 ml) water, plus more as needed

8 ounces (225 g) rotini pasta

MARINARA SAUCE

1 can (14.5 ounces [406 g]) crushed tomatoes

1 tablespoon (7 g) grated fresh carrot

½ teaspoon garlic powder

½ teaspoon dried basil

½ teaspoon salt

Freshly ground black pepper

Red pepper flakes, optional

Tip

The grated carrot adds sweetness and extra vegetables to the sauce; if you'd like, you can add more to your taste or omit it. If you don't want to grate the carrot, you can also roast or boil it and mash it before adding to the marinara sauce.

1 Add the water and rotini to the pressure cooking pot. Make sure the water covers the rotini. Place a trivet on top of the rotini.

2 *Prepare the marinara sauce:* In a 7-inch (18 cm) cake pan, stir together the tomatoes, grated carrot, garlic powder, basil, and salt. Use a sling to lower the pan carefully onto the trivet. Lock the lid in place. Select High Pressure and 4 minutes cook time.

3 When the cook time ends, turn off the pressure cooker. Use a quick pressure release. If foam or liquid begins to come from the steam release valve, close it and wait a minute, then try again. When the float valve drops, carefully remove the lid.

4 Use the sling to remove the pan from the cooking pot. Remove the trivet. Use a slotted spoon to scoop the rotini into bowls. The marinara sauce will continue to thicken as it cools. Season with additional salt, black pepper, or red pepper flakes to taste.

Chicken Risotto and Fresh Vegetables

Cooking risotto is so much easier in the pressure cooker than on the stove. Pressure cooker risotto comes out smooth and creamy and lets you skip all the stirring and adding liquids in batches. This smooth and creamy risotto is loaded with chicken and fresh veggies to make a full meal.

MAKES 4 SERVINGS.

1 large boneless, skinless chicken breast, diced

Salt and freshly ground black pepper

¼ teaspoon dried marjoram, herbes de Provence, rosemary, or basil

4 to 5 tablespoons (55 to 70 g) unsalted butter, divided, plus more if necessary

10 fresh asparagus spears, trimmed and cut into 2-inch (5 cm) pieces

½ medium zucchini, thinly sliced

½ yellow squash, thinly sliced

1 tablespoon (15 ml) olive oil

½ cup (80 g) diced onion

1½ cups (270 g) Arborio rice

1 tablespoon (9 g) capers, optional

2¼ cups (535 ml) reduced-sodium chicken broth

2 to 4 tablespoons (28 to 60 ml) fresh lemon juice

1 tablespoon (6 g) lemon zest

1 cup (80 g) finely shredded Parmesan cheese, plus more for serving

½ cup (55 g) freshly grated fontina cheese

1 tablespoon (1 g) dried parsley

1 Generously season the chicken with salt, pepper, and herbs. Set aside.

2 Select Sauté to preheat the pressure cooking pot. When the pot is hot, melt 1 tablespoon (14 g) butter in the cooking pot. Add the asparagus spears and sauté for 2 minutes. Add the zucchini and squash slices and sauté for 1 minute more. Transfer the vegetables from the pressure cooking pot to a platter and cover.

3 Add 1 tablespoon (14 g) butter and 1 tablespoon (15 ml) oil to the cooking pot. Add the chicken and brown for 2 minutes. Remove the browned chicken to a platter.

4 Add 1 tablespoon (14 g) butter to the pressure cooking pot. Add the onion and cook, stirring often, for about 1 minute. Add the rice and sauté for 3 minutes. Add another 1 tablespoon (14 g) butter if needed. Add the capers (if using), and cook for 1 minute more.

5 Add the chicken broth. Add the chicken with any accumulated juices, lemon juice, and lemon zest. Lock the lid in place. Select High Pressure and 5 minutes cook time.

6 When the cook time ends, turn off the pressure cooker. Use a quick pressure release. When the float valve drops, carefully remove the lid.

7 Stir in the Parmesan and fontina cheese, parsley, and 1 tablespoon (14 g) butter. Stir in the sautéed vegetables and heat through. Serve immediately, topped with additional Parmesan if desired.

Tip

This meal cooks up thick to make it easier for toddlers to eat. If you'd like a thinner consistency, add more chicken broth before serving.

Easy Pork Chops in Gravy

This old-fashioned, family-favorite recipe has been passed down from generation to generation. Our family called it "pork chops the long way" before we updated it for the pressure cooker. The pork chops are so tender, you can use a fork to chop them into bite-size toddler pieces.

MAKES 4 SERVINGS.

4 boneless pork loin chops, about 1 inch (2.5 cm) thick

Lemon pepper or your favorite spice blend, for seasoning

1 tablespoon (15 ml) vegetable oil

2¾ cups (650 ml) water, divided

1 can (10.5 ounces [295 g]) condensed cream of mushroom soup

1 cup (185 g) white rice

2 tablespoons (16 g) all-purpose flour, optional

3 tablespoons (45 ml) cold water, optional

1 Pat the pork chops dry and season liberally with lemon pepper. Select Sauté to preheat the pressure cooking pot. When the pot is hot, add the vegetable oil. Add 2 chops and brown for about 2 minutes per side. Transfer to a platter and repeat with the remaining 2 chops.

2 Add 1½ cups (355ml) water to deglaze the pot, scraping up any browned bits from the bottom. Stir in the mushroom soup. Add the pork chops and any accumulated juices.

3 Place a trivet in the bottom of the pressure cooking pot over the pork chops. In a 7-inch (18 cm) cake pan, stir together the rice and remaining 1¼ cups (295 ml) water. Use a sling to lower the pan carefully onto the trivet. Lock the lid in place. Select High Pressure and 4 minutes cook time.

4 When the cook time ends, turn off the pressure cooker. Let the pressure release naturally for 10 minutes, then finish with a quick pressure release. When the float valve drops, carefully remove the lid. Use the sling to remove the pan from the cooking pot. Remove the trivet. Transfer the pork chops to a large serving bowl.

5 If you prefer a thicker gravy, select Sauté and whisk the flour into the cold water in a small bowl until smooth. Add 1 cup (235 ml) gravy to the flour mixture and stir until well combined. Slowly stir this mixture into the gravy in the cooking pot. Cook, stirring constantly, until thickened to the desired consistency. Pour the gravy over the chops and rice to serve.

Tip

If you prefer a thicker gravy, increase the flour slurry to 4 tablespoons (31 g) flour with 5 tablespoons (75 ml) cold water, then continue with the recipe as directed. Be sure to allow time for the flour to cook over medium heat until bubbly to get the full thickening effect.

Cubed Beef and Gravy over Noodles

These fall-apart-in-your-mouth pieces of sirloin and flavorful gravy are served over egg noodles. Adding sour cream is optional, but many toddlers love the flavor and even use it as a dip for steamed veggies.

MAKES 4 SERVINGS.

1 to 2 tablespoons (15 to 28 ml) vegetable oil

2 pounds (900 g) beef sirloin tip roast, cubed

¼ cup (40 g) finely diced onion

1 cup (235 ml) reduced-sodium beef broth

1 cube beef bouillon, optional

¼ to ½ cup (31 to 63 g) all-purpose flour

1 cup (235 ml) warm water

Salt and freshly ground black pepper

1 package (16 ounces [455 g]) egg noodles, cooked according to package directions

Worcestershire sauce, for serving, optional

Sour cream, for serving, optional

1 Select Sauté and preheat the pressure cooking pot. When the pot is hot, add 1 tablespoon (15 ml) oil and brown the meat on one side in small batches, adding more oil if needed; do not crowd the pot. Transfer all the browned meat to a plate, then add the onion to the cooking pot and sauté until tender, about 1 minute.

2 Add the beef broth and beef bouillon (if using) to the cooking pot. Add the browned beef and any juices that may have accumulated. Lock the lid in place. Select High Pressure and 15 minutes cook time.

3 When the cook time ends, turn off the pressure cooker. Use a quick pressure release. When the float valve drops, carefully remove the lid.

4 In a small bowl, mix flour and 1 cup (235 ml) warm water to make a slurry to thicken the broth. Stirring constantly, add the slurry to the cooking pot. Select Sauté and bring to a boil. Boil for a few minutes, until the gravy is thickened. Add salt and pepper to taste.

5 Serve the beef and gravy over the prepared egg noodles. Top with a splash of Worcestershire sauce and a dollop of sour cream, if desired.

Tip

If you want, you can substitute 1 tablespoon (5 g) dehydrated onion for the diced onion. Just add it with the beef broth after browning the beef.

Creamy Chicken and Rice Soup

This creamy soup is made very thick so it's easier for toddlers to eat and features classic flavors the whole family is sure to love.

MAKES 4 SERVINGS.

1 tablespoon (14 g) unsalted butter

½ cup (80 g) chopped onion

½ cup (65 g) diced carrot

½ cup (60 g) diced celery

1 large boneless, skinless chicken breast, diced

2½ cups (570 ml) reduced-sodium chicken broth

6 ounces (170 g) Uncle Ben's Original White Rice

1 tablespoon (1 g) dried parsley

½ teaspoon salt

½ teaspoon freshly ground black pepper

Dash of red pepper flakes, optional

2 tablespoons (16 g) cornstarch

2 tablespoons (28 ml) cold water

3 ounces (85 g) cream cheese, cubed

¼ cup (60 ml) milk

¼ cup (60 ml) half-and-half

Tip

If you prefer, you can thin the adult portions of the soup. After you've removed your toddler's meal, add another ¼ cup (60 ml) milk and ¼ cup (60 ml) half-and-half, then add more chicken broth to reach the desired consistency.

1 Select Sauté to preheat the pressure cooking pot. When the pot is hot, add the butter to melt. Add the onion, carrot, and celery. Sauté for about 5 minutes, stirring occasionally, until the vegetables are tender. Stir in the chicken, chicken broth, rice, parsley, salt, pepper, and red pepper flakes (if using). Lock the lid in place. Select High Pressure and 5 minutes cook time.

2 When the cook time ends, turn off the pressure cooker. Let the pressure release naturally for 5 minutes, then finish with a quick pressure release. When the float valve drops, carefully remove the lid.

3 In a small bowl, whisk the cornstarch and 2 tablespoons (28 ml) cold water until smooth. Select Sauté and add the slurry to the pot, stirring constantly. Stir in the cream cheese until melted. Stir in the milk and half-and-half and heat through—do not bring to a boil.

Mild Cilantro Chicken and Avocado Soup

A chunky chicken soup made with mild chili peppers and served over white rice is a great way to introduce toddlers to different ethnic foods.

MAKES 4 SERVINGS.

SOFRITO

3 tablespoons (45 ml) olive oil, divided

1 pasilla or poblano chili pepper, stemmed, seeded, and chopped

1 medium onion, diced

10 cloves garlic, minced or pressed

1 bunch fresh cilantro

SOUP

1 tablespoon (15 ml) olive oil

4 boneless, skinless chicken thighs, cut into bite-size pieces

4¼ cups (1 L) water, divided

1 tablespoon (12 g) Caldo de Tomate seasoning, or substitute for 1 bouillon cube and 1 table-spoon (16 g) tomato paste

1 cup (185 g) white rice

1½ tablespoons (23 ml) apple cider vinegar

Diced avocado, for serving

1 *Prepare the sofrito:* Select Sauté to preheat the pressure cooking pot. When the pot is hot, add 1 tablespoon (15 ml) oil and sauté the pepper, onion, and garlic for 3 to 5 minutes, until tender. Turn off pressure cooker and transfer the mixture to a blender. Add the cilantro and remaining 2 tablespoons oil (28 ml). Blend until the mixture is the consistency of pesto.

2 *Prepare the soup:* Select Sauté to preheat the pressure cooking pot. When the pot is hot, add the oil and brown the chicken for 3 minutes. Add 3 cups (700 ml) water and the seasoning to the pressure cooking pot and stir to dissolve. Place a trivet in the pot over the chicken.

3 In a 7-inch (18 cm) round cake pan, add the rice and remaining 1¼ cups (295 ml) water. Using a sling, carefully lower the pan onto the trivet. Lock the lid in place. Select High Pressure and 4 minutes cook time.

4 When the cook time ends, turn off the pressure cooker. Allow the pressure to release naturally for 10 minutes, then finish with a quick pressure release. When the float valve drops, carefully remove the lid.

5 Use the sling to remove the pan from the pot. Remove the trivet. Add a quarter of the sofrito mixture and the apple cider vinegar to the liquid in the pressure cooking pot. Select Sauté and simmer for 10 minutes.

6 To serve, add a scoop of rice to soup bowls and ladle the soup over the top. Garnish with the avocado.

Tip

The extra sofrito can be stored for up to 1 month. Use it to make another batch of soup—it freezes well—or to make other Mexican-inspired dishes. We like to stir it into fresh rice and serve as a side for tacos.

Chapter 9

Toddler-Friendly Desserts

We don't always serve desserts, but when we want to celebrate a special occasion or milestone, these desserts are easy, fun, and toddler-friendly!

Recipes

Apple-Berry-Cherry Crisp

Fruit fillings are quick and easy to make in the pressure cooker. By cooking the fruit in the pressure cooker before crisping up the topping in the oven, you cut the cook time by about half.

MAKES 4 SERVINGS.

Nonstick baking spray with flour

4 baking apples, such as Braeburn or Golden Delicious, peeled, cored, and sliced into ¼-inch (6 mm) slices

3 to 4 cups (700 to 946 ml) boiling water

2 cups (310 g) frozen blueberries

1 cup (156 g) frozen cherries

¼ cup (50 g) granulated sugar

1 tablespoon (15 ml) lemon juice

3 tablespoons (24 g) cornstarch

3 tablespoons (45 ml) water

TOPPING

¼ cup (31 g) all-purpose flour

¼ teaspoon salt

¼ cup (55 g) brown sugar

4 tablespoons (55 g) unsalted butter, cut into small pieces

1 cup (80 g) instant rolled oats

Vanilla ice cream, optional, for serving

1 Preheat the oven to 375°F (190°C, or gas mark 5). Coat an 8 x 8-inch (20 x 20 cm) pan with nonstick baking spray with flour.

2 Place the apple slices in a large bowl or pot. Pour the boiling water directly over the top of the apples. Cover and let sit for 10 minutes. Transfer the apples to a colander and drain well, tossing occasionally until completely dry, about 10 minutes.

3 While the apples are soaking, add the blueberries, cherries, granulated sugar, and lemon juice to the pressure cooking pot, and stir to combine. Lock the lid in place and select High Pressure and 2 minutes cook time. When the cook time ends, turn off the pressure cooker. Allow the pressure to release naturally for 10 minutes, then finish with a quick pressure release.

4 In a small bowl, whisk together the cornstarch and water. Add the slurry and apples to the pressure cooking pot. Bring to a boil using the Sauté function, stirring constantly. Sauté for 2 minutes.

5 *Prepare the topping:* Meanwhile, in a large bowl, combine the flour, salt, and brown sugar. Using a pastry blender, cut in the butter until large clumps form. Mix in the oats. Set aside.

6 Pour the fruit mixture into the prepared baking dish. Sprinkle the topping mixture evenly on the filling. Place the baking dish on a rimmed baking sheet and bake until the topping is golden brown, about 4 minutes. Let rest for a few minutes before serving.

7 Serve warm, topped with a scoop of vanilla ice cream, if desired.

Tip

To reheat, simply place in a covered bowl and microwave at 50 percent power in 30-second intervals until it reaches your desired temperature.

Fresh Berries and Vanilla Cream

Having fresh fruit for dessert is a great habit to start. Drizzling a small scoop of the vanilla cream over the fruit will have your toddler asking for berries for dessert often!

MAKES 4 SERVINGS.

¾ cup (175 ml) heavy cream

¼ cup (60 ml) milk

2 egg yolks

⅓ cup (67 g) sugar

1 teaspoon vanilla bean paste or extract

4 cups in-season fresh berries ([680 g] sliced strawberries, [500 g] raspberries, [580 g] blueberries, [580 g] blackberries)

Tip

If your pressure cooker does not adjust to a low heat Sauté setting, you will get best results cooking the vanilla cream on your stovetop.

1 Select Sauté on your pressure cooker and adjust to low. In the pressure cooking pot, whisk the heavy cream and milk. Cook until the mixture just starts to boil. Remove from the heat.

2 In a medium-size bowl, whisk the egg yolks and sugar until the mixture is pale and thick. Whisk in half the hot milk mixture. Add the egg mixture to the pressure cooking pot, stirring constantly, until the sauce comes to a boil. Turn off the pressure cooker and simmer for about 2 minutes more, stirring constantly. Remove the cooking pot from the housing and stir in the vanilla.

3 Transfer the vanilla cream to a serving bowl or gravy boat and allow to cool. To serve, place berries in small serving dishes and drizzle vanilla cream over the top.

Alex's Brownie Pops

Apologies to fans of edge pieces—brownies made in the pressure cooker are all middle-piece fudgy chocolate. These rich, moist brownies are perfect for a fun, bite-size treat!

MAKES 18 TO 20 BROWNIE POPS

Nonstick baking spray with flour

1 box (about 20 ounces [560 g]) family-size fudgy brownie mix (we use Ghirardelli Triple Chocolate)

18 to 20 lollipop sticks

12 to 16 ounces (340 to 454 g) milk, semisweet, or dark chocolate (we use melting wafers)

Sprinkles, jimmies, or colorful candy melts, for decoration

Tip

This treat is fun to decorate with your toddler! To reduce mess, put your toddler in charge of sprinkles and place the dipped brownie pops on a lined baking sheet. If your toddler insists on dipping, be aware that you may need more melted chocolate because toddlers tend to dip the chocolate liberally.

1 Coat a 7-inch (18 cm) springform pan with nonstick baking spray with flour. Set aside.

2 Prepare the brownie mix as directed on the packaging, using the recommended oil, water, and eggs for fudgy brownies. (If you're at altitude, be sure to follow the high-altitude directions.) Pour the batter into the prepared pan.

3 Pour 1 cup (235 ml) water into the pressure cooking pot and place a trivet in the bottom. Carefully center the filled pan on a sling and lower the uncovered pan onto the trivet. Lock the lid in place. Select High Pressure and 43 minutes cook time.

4 When the cook time ends, turn off the pressure cooker. Let the pressure release naturally for 15 minutes, then finish with a quick pressure release. When the float valve drops, carefully remove the lid. Test the brownies for doneness, either when a toothpick comes out clean or when the brownies spring back when touched gently. Use the sling to transfer the pan to a wire rack and use a paper towel to soak up any water that may have accumulated on top of the brownies or around the sides of the springform pan.

5 Cool for 5 minutes, then slide a thin spatula or knife around the edge of the springform pan to loosen the brownies and open the springform pan. Allow to cool for at least 1 hour.

6 Remove the baked brownies to a large bowl and use a large spoon or your hands to crumble the brownies. Use a #40 cookie scoop (about 1½ tablespoons [23 g]) to scoop brownies into balls. Roll with your hands to smooth out the balls and place on a lined baking sheet. Insert a lollipop stick into each brownie ball. Freeze for at least 2 hours or overnight.

7 When ready to decorate, in a microwave-safe dish, heat chocolate on 50 percent power for 1 minute, then stir. Continue melting and stirring in 30-second intervals until the chocolate is fully melted and smooth.

8 Dip a brownie pop into the melted chocolate. If necessary, use a spoon to completely coat the pop with chocolate and let the excess chocolate drip back into the bowl. Place on the prepared baking sheet. Scatter sprinkles on the chocolate while it is still wet. Repeat with the remaining pops. If the chocolate starts to thicken as it cools, return to the microwave for 15 seconds at 50 percent power. Refrigerate the dipped brownie pops until ready to serve.

Acknowledgments

First, I want to thank all my *Pressure Cooking Today* readers and members of the various Facebook communities, who share their enthusiasm for pressure cooking with me. They keep me energized and striving to create new and innovative recipes and to find new ways to use the electric pressure cooker.

Thank you to my publisher for seeing the need for making baby and toddler food quickly and easily in an electric pressure cooker.

Thanks to my husband, who is my indispensable slicer and dicer in the kitchen. He makes recipe creation so much easier, and he makes it more fun to cook.

Finally, thanks to my amazing, talented daughter who put her heart and soul into this cookbook. She spent hours researching dietary recommendations for babies so that the recipes are based on the most up-to-date information available to use with her new daughter. I have enjoyed writing this book with her and am proud to welcome her to my blog.

— BARBARA

This book wouldn't be possible without my family, and I am deeply grateful for them.

First and foremost, to my mother, for your unfailing belief that someone as distracted as me could ever be a good cook. Thank you for inviting me to help in your kitchen and with your websites. I am so grateful for the opportunities you've provided me and am thrilled to join you on this pressure cooking journey.

To my father, for being happy to help however needed, from lending a hand in the kitchen to watching my boys so I could write.

To my boys, for happily suggesting recipe ideas, taste-testing recipes, and providing candid feedback. Thank you for eating toddler meals for breakfast, lunch, and dinner and having baby foods for snacks and dessert. I love watching you grow and can't wait to see what you do next.

To my husband, whose contributions to this cookbook are innumerable and whose steady support made it possible. You are truly my partner on this journey, and I just adore you.

And finally, to my baby girl, who arrived right in the middle of writing this cookbook and snuggled with me throughout the editing process. I can't wait to share these recipes with you! You were absolutely worth the wait!

— JENNIFER

About the Authors

Barbara Schieving *(left)* is a veteran mom of four grown children. She is widely admired cook, writer, and photographer whose two blogs, *Pressure Cooking Today* and *Barbara Bakes*, delight more than 1.5 million readers each month with her fabulous, family-friendly recipes and conversational style. Her most recent cookbook, *Instantly Sweet* (2018), written with Marci Buttars, introduces readers to the sweet side of electric pressure cooking, with 75 delicious desserts and sweet treats. Her other cookbooks include *The Electric Pressure Cooker Cookbook* (2017), which features 200 delicious recipes made pressure-cooker-fast with fresh and familiar ingredients, and *Simply Sweet Dream Puffs* (2015), which features a wide variety of easy-to-make cream puffs, eclairs, and profiteroles. She lives in the Salt Lake City, Utah area.

Jennifer Schieving McDaniel is a busy mother of three. She fell in love with pressure cooking when she and her husband lived with her parents while building a new home and is now a huge pressure cooker enthusiast. She uses her pressure cooker every day, often several times a day, to prepare nutritious family meals and can't wait to make these recipes for the little one who recently joined their family. Jennifer and her husband love sharing their pressure cooking expertise and often teach friends, family, and groups how easy it is to cook great meals in the pressure cooker. Jennifer is the managing editor for *Pressure Cooking Today* and is an integral part of *Pressure Cooking Today* team. She creates recipes, writes how-to posts, answers readers' questions, and so much more. She lives near Barbara in the Salt Lake City, Utah area.

Index

Index